Carpentry for Beginners: Things to Make

John Duncan Adams

CARPENTRY
FOR BEGINNERS

THINGS TO MAKE

BY

JOHN D. ADAMS
Author of "When Mother Lets Us Carpenter," etc.

ILLUSTRATED WITH SKETCHES AND DIAGRAMS BY THE AUTHOR

NEW YORK
MOFFAT, YARD AND COMPANY
1917

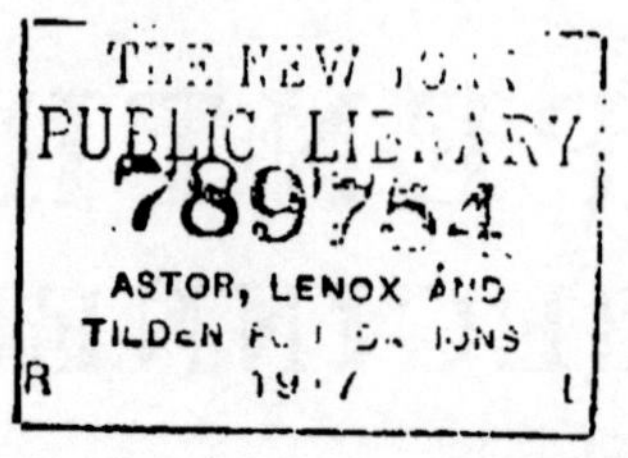

Published September, 1917

FOREWORD

There is no lack of textbooks telling the amateur carpenter with mathematical exactness just how to make a dovetail joint or a mortise and tenon connection. The beginner has no difficulty in finding simple instruction as to the theory of carpentry, and may read at great length precisely how to hold the hammer or manipulate a plane. With this phase of the subject the present volume has no concern. It is not expected that those to whom the book is addressed aim to become professional carpenters. The object of the volume is merely to present as clearly as possible an interesting and practical field to the young craftsman, and this is sufficient for the reason that if the work is made interesting he will soon find out all he needs to know about tools, and if the results are of practical value he will not lack encouragement.

By presenting a great variety of articles ranging from the simplest to those in the construction of which some little assistance may be required, it is hoped that the book will be of interest to young and old, experienced and unexperienced alike.

In the fore part will be found the more simple

articles. As these are the pieces the young carpenter will attempt, the drawings have been prepared accordingly. Here the customary working drawings of the assembled article, with their numerous dimension lines, have been omitted. Each piece of wood, however, is delineated separately on a series of squares, which not only display the necessary measurements, but show the relation of the various lines all at a glance. The idea of proportion is thus accentuated and in a way would be impossible were the dimensional data displayed numerically instead of graphically.

As the more elaborate articles are taken up, however, this method is not only impracticable on account of the number of pieces involved, but is unnecessary to the more advanced workers. But even here the text may appear too detailed to those having training in woodworking, but the amateur will do well to follow the instructions closely, as the successful completion of a piece of furniture will largely depend on the order of preparing the various parts.

Many of the structural details involved are not, of course, such as would generally be practiced in a factory where all manner of woodworking machinery is at hand, but are planned so that the beginner, with ordinary tools in good condition, will encounter as little difficulty as possible.

TO THE HOME CARPENTER

If there is one DON'T that should be impressed more than any other on the mind of the amateur carpenter it is DON'T HURRY. Before touching a single piece of wood be sure you know exactly what is required and what you are going to do. Success in this sort of work lies in not starting until you have a clear and vivid mental picture of each part of the thing you are going to make and not stopping until you have made it look exactly like that picture.

Mark out the necessary lines with a sharp pencil, and as you cut away the extra wood, forget all about the other pieces, and work on the one in hand just as though everything depended on IT. If you have an interest in what you are doing and will not hurry or become impatient, there can only be one result and that will be delightfully surprising.

One should remember that wood seldom comes from the mill exactly according to stated measurements, so that it is always advisable to prepare the principal pieces first and then accurately fit the others in place as the work proceeds.

DIMENSIONS

All figures refer to dimensions in inches, and the conventional sign has accordingly been omitted.

In the squared diagrams each of the small squares represents exactly one inch.

MATERIAL

The most satisfactory wood for making the many useful little articles described in the fore part of this book is soft pine. This wood is inexpensive, cuts easily and may be had quite free from knots. Often some suitable material may be had by taking apart grocery boxes, although these are frequently planed smooth only on the outside. The best plan is to go to the planing mill, where one can usually get quite a little stock of odds and ends at a very small cost. Among these there should be a few small boards of assorted thicknesses, such as one-quarter, three-eighths and half inch stuff.

For the larger pieces oak is the most desirable and durable wood, particularly for furniture. Mahogany and walnut are beautiful woods, but are so expensive as to render their use prohibitive. Poplar is a wood that works easily and may often be used to good advantage in the construction of drawers and other parts of furniture not usually exposed. Cedar also works easily and takes a fine finish, but is readily marred.

Before beginning the construction of the larger pieces the drawings and descriptions should be carefully studied, and a list of the necessary pieces separately made out, so that they may all be ordered at once. This will result in securing a more uniform stock, both as to grade and thickness.

Always keep a good assortment of brads and finishing nails on hand. Never use old bent nails. They are difficult to drive straight, and new ones cost only a few cents a pound. Many a piece has been split by attempting to use a nail that is not the proper size.

Sandpaper in different degrees of fineness should also be kept in stock.

TOOLS

The adjoining page shows the principal tools required. For most of the simple pieces one can get along quite well with only a hammer, saw and a sharp knife. Do not under any circumstances buy a box of cheap tools simply because there are a great many of them, for it is always much better to buy good tools one at a time as one can afford them.

A good carborundum stone that cuts rápidly and an oil stone for finishing will later be found very necessary, as it is impossible to do good work and make reasonable progress with dull tools. As the work proceeds a bench having a carpenter's vise will be found a great convenience. Manual training supply houses now furnish small benches that embody many useful features and take up but little room.

A glue pot, with an outer water jacket to prevent burning, while not necessary, simplifies the preparation of glue, and a pair of wooden screw clamps are almost indispensable where a strong joint is desired.

TABLE OF CONTENTS

CONTENTS

CONTENTS

CONTENTS

CARPENTRY FOR BEGINNERS

CHAPTER 1

Staining and Finishing

Pine can be stained to closely match almost any of the more expensive and harder woods of which furniture is generally made. The hardware stores supply color cards that show the effect of their stains, which may be had in small cans and are easily applied. There are three kinds of stains sold —water, acid, and oil stain. Always use the latter, which may be applied with a brush or a rag, rubbing it well in and finally wiping off with a dry cloth all that has not soaked in. Always try the stain on a small block before using.

After the piece has thoroughly dried, which will take several hours, go over the surface very lightly with fine sandpaper, and then apply a coat of rubbing wax, which also comes in small cans and is about as thick as shoe polish. Rub this in evenly

all over, rubbing with the grain and real hard for several minutes.

This simple process results in a very practical finish, which may easily be restored when scratched by rewaxing.

The foregoing answers very well for the more simple pieces, but with pieces of furniture that are to be used daily for years a more elaborate treatment is necessary.

While accurate building is, of course, the essential requirement, an otherwise successful article may be quite ruined by being poorly finished. A piece well constructed, substantially built, the grain of the wood accurately matched, the parts soundly fitted together and the general line of the article artistic, needs to be properly finished to make it a truly successful piece of work.

Before beginning the finishing of a new piece of furniture one of the most important points contributing to success is to have the wood in good condition, thoroughly dry and as smooth as it is possible to make it by the use of fine sandpaper. Another feature that contributes greatly to satisfactory results is rubbing, long and steady; in fact, the more rubbing the furniture gets, the more beautiful will be the texture and gloss of the wood, no matter what variety of finish it may receive. Broad surfaces, of course, show the effect of rubbing more than the small parts and the tendency usually is to put a great deal of time on them, but in really good work every part of a piece should have a smooth, satiny texture.

Briefly stated, the method of treating a new piece of furniture involves three operations—namely, staining, filling and finishing. The stain, or wood dye, as it is sometimes called, is applied first and gives the wood the desired shade or color. When the stain is well dried a coat of filler is applied to fill up the pores of the wood, after which the finishing preparation of wax or varnish is put on, one or more coats being used, each carefully rubbed.

Although this has been essentially the method of wood finishing for many years, great progress has recently been made in developing a wide variety of color effects and finishing products that give a durable and elastic, semi-glossy surface. Almost every one is familiar with the exquisite results that may be obtained on such woods as mahogany and oak, but few realize the attractive effects that can be obtained with such inexpensive woods as pine, cypress and chestnut.

Staining.—It will be understood, of course, that an application of stain is only to be made where it is desired to alter the shade or color of the wood. Several of the darker woods look very well when finished natural, and ash and white maple are sometimes kept purposely light.

In selecting a stain consult the actual wood samples usually supplied by manufacturers to the stores handling their products. If the stain has to be ordered by mail, send for the color-plates showing the actual effect on the wood before ordering. Carefully note whether the color effect selected was obtained on hard or soft wood, because the softer the wood, the more stain it will absorb, and the more stain it takes, the darker the resultant shade. This, however, may be easily remedied by thinning the stain with alcohol, gasolene or turpentine, as required by the directions on the can. The latter is necessary if it is an oil stain, which variety is the most easily applied for the reason that it dries more slowly. In any case it is safer when working with a new product to experiment with a block of the actual wood or on the under side of the article to be finished. Be sure that all drops of glue have been removed and that the surface is smooth and without greasy finger-marks. Handle the brush in an orderly manner, and do not paint a part simply because it happens to be near the brush.

If, for instance, you are staining the square leg of a table, start at the top of one side and complete that side before starting another, taking due care not to carry the brush so full as to cause the stain to trickle around the edges onto the new wood. The best brush for handling thin stains is that known as the fitch-brush. In such woods as Oregon pine or redwood, the grain may be greatly intensified by wiping off the surplus stain with a soft cloth before it has had time to soak into the more resinous portions of the wood.

When the stain has thoroughly dried, which will take from eighteen to twenty-four hours, it will be found that the wood feels rough and that the stain has raised the grain. This is soon remedied, however, by rubbing lightly with OO sandpaper, which, if held in the hand without a block, will give a smoother surface than ever. If, after wiping off the dust with a soft rag, it is found that more contrast or a darker shade is desired, apply a second coat of the stain.

Filling.—Wood fillers are made in two forms—paste and liquid. The former is used principally for open-grained woods such as chestnut, oak and ash, and the latter for soft woods such as whitewood, pine or cypress. The filler may be had in a variety of colors resembling the different woods, and also without any coloring matter, in which case it is called "natural" or "transparent" filler. The filler should be about the consistency of flowing varnish and be applied with a brush, thoroughly rubbing it into the pores of the wood. After five or ten minutes, when the gloss will have deadened, wipe off the surplus with a soft rag and then allow the piece to stand overnight. If the filler is found to be quick-drying, then only a small section of the surface should be covered at a time so that the surplus may be wiped off readily. The filler is only intended to fill the pores of the wood and should be wiped off against the grain. With open-grained woods, such as oak and chestnut, the most beautiful effects may be obtained by using a light filler, which does not affect the general color, but merely brings out the fine texture and flake of the wood.

Quite often the staining and filling can be done more advantageously while the piece of furniture is in sections. For example, a table before the final assembling may consist of the top, the two complete ends, and the foot-board—four sections, all of which can be stained and filled before putting together, thus leaving only the finishing to be done after the table is finally set up. In chairs and other articles requiring upholstering most, if not all, of the finishing may be done before the leather or other material is attached.

Finishing.—The wood is now of the proper color and presents a smooth and continuous surface, which must now be protected by means of the finishing coat. The most easily handled finishing material is prepared wax, which is put up in various sized cans and can be well applied with a soft cloth. The polishing may commence about fifteen minutes after applying. It is usually done with a polishing-mitt, although a dry cloth will answer the purpose quite as well. No particular care is necessary in putting on the wax, as any overlapping does not show after polishing.

There are many excellent finishing preparations on the market having wax in composition, which are sold under suggestive trade names. These are usually applied with a brush, and are put up in various sized cans, upon which will be found any special directions required in applying them.

Should it be desired to secure a rather harder and more impervious surface than that afforded by a single application of wax, a coat of thin shellac may be applied before waxing or applying the finishing coat. Pure shellac varnish—that is, dry shellac dissolved in grain alcohol—is very quick-drying and is therefore a rather troublesome material to apply uniformly, particularly on a large surface. There are, however, many preparations marketed under fancy names that serve the same purpose as shellac and can be much more easily applied. After this coat has thoroughly dried go over the surface with the finest sandpaper obtainable before applying the filler.

The high polishes so popular in the past were secured by the use of varnish, which is a resinous substance incorporated with oils, turpentine, etc. After each coat the surface is thoroughly rubbed with pulverized pumice-stone and linseed-oil. The dull, wax-like finishes, however, are now meeting general favor, deservedly so, for the reason that the surface may be freshened up at any time by a few minutes' application of the polishing-mitt.

Fuming.—One of the most popular finishes among craftsmen is the rich nut-brown shade known as "fumed oak"—a finish that will harmonize with almost any scheme of interior decoration. In producing the genuine finish, the white oak is placed in air-tight receptacles containing pans of ammonia, the fumes from which enter the pores and effect a chemical change in the tannic acid, which is prominent in this wood. After a day or so the wood is discolored to a considerable depth and is ready for the filling preparation.

When the amateur goes to the paint-store to purchase the necessary supplies, he will be rather surprised, if not positively confused, at the great variety of preparations bearing elaborate names with which he will be totally unacquainted. But keeping in mind the fact that these are only names for a filler, a varnish or a wax preparation, he will not experience much difficulty in getting exactly what is wanted.

Puttying.—No good carpenter ever uses very much putty, but when one is just starting there is sure to be a crack or a seam, as well as some nail holes, that will require filling in. Always work up the putty in the hand until it is soft and free from lumps. Never attempt to apply it to new wood, because the wood will absorb the oil and the putty will crumble out. See that the oil stain runs well into the places to be puttied and also work up a little stain with the putty so that it will match the wood. Never apply the putty until the wood is perfectly dry.

CHAPTER 2

Things for the Little Ones to Make

MAKING A SWING BOARD

"A swing board," you say, "that's easy. Who doesn't know how to make a swing board?" Of course it is easy, and because it is so it is a good example to show that even in the making of the simplest things there is a right way and a wrong way. The usual way is to cut a V-shaped nick in each end, and, every time any one jumps off, the board falls into the trampled dust below. Here is the right way:

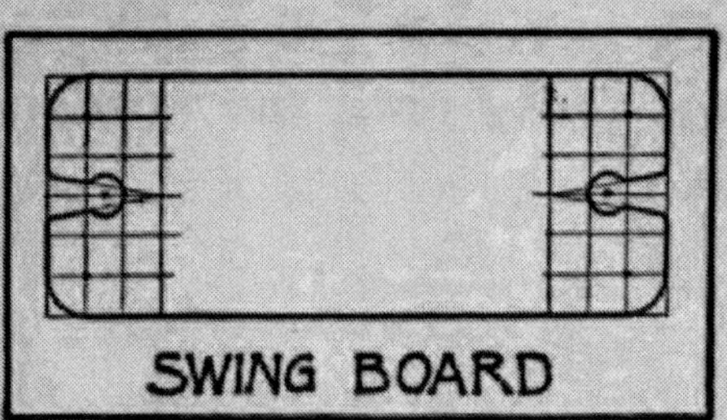

Get a board about six inches wide and as long as the ropes are apart at the top of the swing. Square off the ends with the saw and then draw some one-inch squares as shown in the drawing.

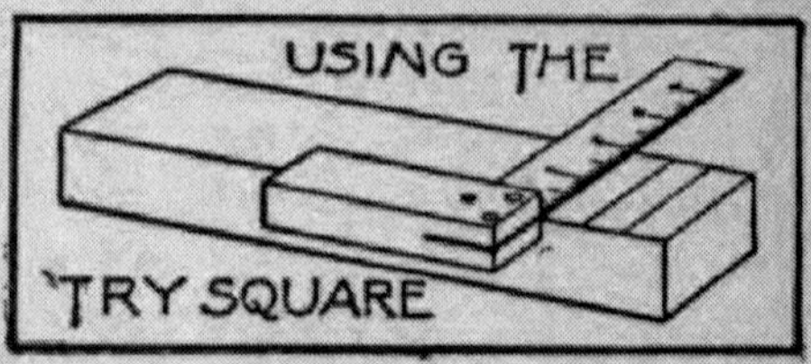

Next take the compasses and draw the circles for the rope and the curve at each corner, placing the point of the compasses exactly on the points marked with the black dots in the drawing. Bore the two holes for the rope and saw out the tapering piece at each end so that the rope can just be forced into the holes. Round off the corners, sandpaper the edges and you will have a board that will not catch and tear or fall off.

COAT HANGER

A coat hanger is another simple thing to make—provided you go at it in the right way. A paper pattern should first be made, and for this we will need a piece of smooth wrapping paper large

enough for us to mark out three rows of one-inch squares, fifteen squares to the row. Tack this down and then tie a piece of string to a lead pencil in order to draw the two curves, which is a very easy matter when the other end of the string is tied or looped around a tack. For the top curve the string should be thirteen inches long and nineteen for the lower. In order to place the curves properly on the squares, keep shifting the tack until the two ends come out just right. We must now get a piece of wood about three quarters of an inch thick and fifteen inches long, and mark out the pattern on it. The hanger is then to be carefully sawn out with the keyhole saw, after which the edges should be planed smooth and rounded off and the whole piece finally gone over with sandpaper. Next bore a small hole in the center at the top, and then make a hook out of good stout wire, the end of which should be pushed through the hole and bent over to keep it from coming out, after which a coat of thin shellac will complete the task.

SOAP HOLDER

We must now try our skill at making something

consisting of more than one piece, and see how closely the different parts may be fitted together. A good example to begin with is the soap holder illustrated. From the working drawing may be learned all the necessary sizes when it is remembered that each of the small squares represents exactly one inch. The wood should be about three-eighths of an inch thick. First saw out the back, neatly rounding the two upper corners and boring two quarter-inch holes for hanging. Next prepare the front piece, and see that it is exactly the same length as the back. Both pieces should be sandpapered smooth and flat on the ends. Do not hold the sandpaper in the hand, but wrap it on a small flat block, or you will surely rub off too much on one side and so spoil the outline. The two ends are now to be marked out, using a sharp pencil and the square, and finished accurately to line, after

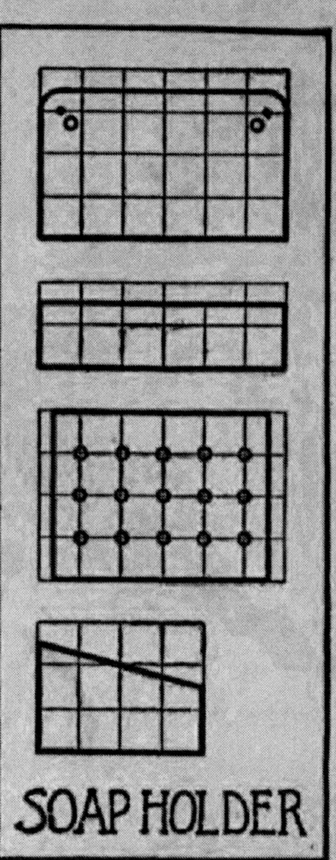

which the four pieces may be nailed together, using two or three small wire nails for each connection. The bottom is now to be sawn out just large enough to fit inside. Bore a number of quarter-inch holes in this, as shown in the working drawing, and then nail in place.

Before using the holder it should be well oiled, and may also be painted with white oil paint to good advantage.

PECK MEASURE

What boy or girl is there who, when sent to buy a peck of apples, has not felt as though peck measures were getting smaller all the time? If you will read what follows and study the drawing, you will be able to make an accurate measure of your own and will then know exactly what you are getting.

You will require some long strips measuring half an inch thick and about an inch and an eighth wide. There will be ten side pieces twelve inches long, three bottom pieces eleven inches, eight end pieces eight inches, and four corner pieces six and three-quarter inches long. For sawing a lot of small pieces like these, it is rather slow to mark each one out with the square, and so carpenters usually have what they call a miter box, which is simply three boards nailed or screwed together so as to form a trough about four inches wide and about two feet long. Two pairs of saw cuts are then made in the sides—one at right angles to the length and the other at forty-five degrees, which is the angle the pieces must be cut when we want to make a picture frame. When you have a miter box and wish to saw a piece off squarely, it is only necessary to place it in the box, hold it tightly against one side and then work the saw back and forth in the slits cut in the sides.

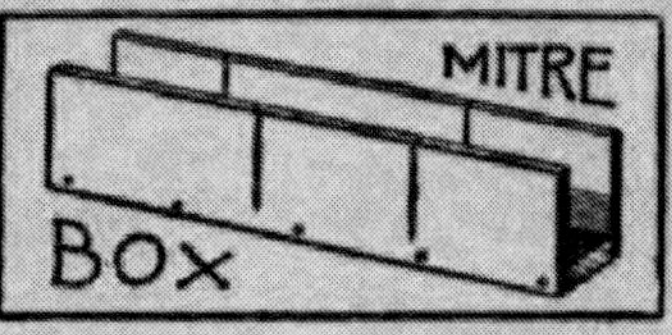

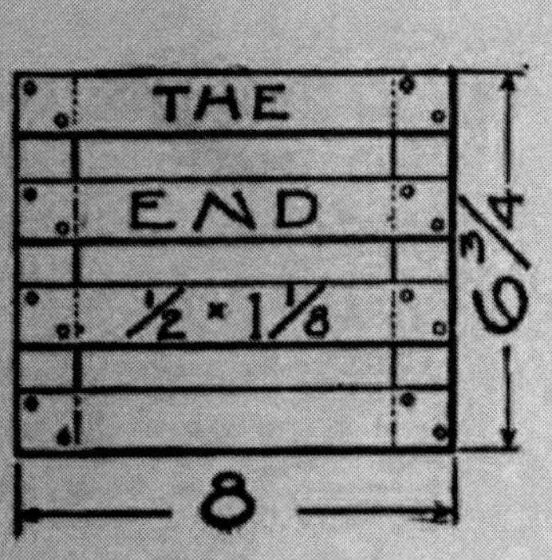

This is a very handy device, and if you make one, take it to the nearest carpenter and he will be glad to saw the slits for you in just the proper places.

After you have cut all the pieces of the crate to the proper length, nail up each end complete as illustrated. Next set up the ends and connect them by nailing on the top and bottom strips of each side, after which it takes but a few minutes to nail on the remaining pieces.

If you should attempt to make this crate out of strips not exactly the size given, some allowance must be made in the length of the side pieces, as the inside dimensions must not be changed.

TOOL BOX

It may be a slat on the chicken coop is broken, perhaps a picket on the front fence is loose or something is wrong with the wireless outfit on the top of the barn — but whatever it is you will find it a great convenience to have a box with a handle so that you can carry the necessary tools and nails to where they are needed to make repairs.

There are six pieces of wood in the box illustrated, and you will get a clear idea of their sizes and shapes from the working drawing, in which each small square represents exactly one inch. The boards should be one-half inch thick, but if they are a little thicker it will not matter, provided you proceed in the proper order.

First saw the side and end pieces off squarely to the exact length. Nail these together and then measure the size of the bottom, which should next be nailed on. The center piece is six inches wide and should now be cut just long enough to fit in snugly between the ends. Mark out the upper part as shown in the drawing, but before cutting off the triangle at each of the upper corners, bore two one-inch holes and cut out the wood in between them, so as to form the handle. Nail this piece in place, exactly in the center, driving the nails in through the ends and up through the bottom.

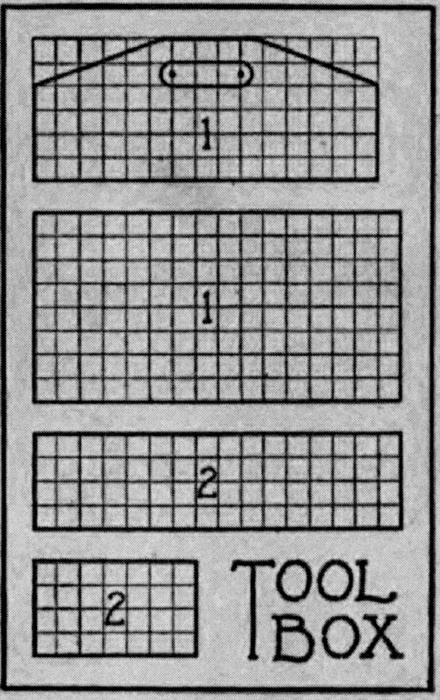

Sometimes these boxes are divided up on one side with several thin cross partitions, so as to form a number of pockets for the different sizes of nails and screws that are generally used. If such a box is desired, one of the sides must be left off until the small partitions are securely fastened in place by nailing in through the center board.

A box for holding knives and forks in the kitchen may be made in the same way as the plain tool box, except that it is not so large and the wood is thinner.

THE BENCH HOOK

In sawing small pieces such as the side boards of the tool box just described, it is often more convenient to saw them on the work-bench instead of holding them on a box with the knee. To do this one must have what is called a bench hook. The way it is used is clearly illustrated, but its full advantage cannot be appreciated until it is tried.

WHAT THE BENCH HOOK IS FOR·

It consists of a small board about four inches wide and eight inches long with a little cross-strip nailed squarely across each end—one on top and one below. The lower one catches the edge of the bench and the top one keeps the board being sawn from slipping back. When one attempts to hold a piece of wood on the bench while it is being sawn, it will almost always shift back and forth with the saw, because there is nothing to push against, but with the bench hook one can lean slightly forward and very easily hold the wood steadily against the back piece of the hook.

CANDLE HOLDER AND CANDLE-STICKS

Our little problems thus far have largely been a matter of getting ready. We must now get right down to business and make something just as neatly as we can, so that when it is stained and rubbed it will look good enough to stand on the side-board. Let us try the little candle holder.

First get a hard lead pencil and make it quite sharp. Carefully mark out the base board on a smooth piece of wood, making the corners exactly true by means of the square. Saw this out and then make the edges smooth by means of a piece of sandpaper wrapped on a small flat block. (Never use the sand-paper without the block if you want the edges to be flat and the corners sharp.) Hold it flat and rub back and forth without rocking from side to side, otherwise you will spoil the outline. If you have no vise to hold the wood in place, brace it against some projection to aid you in holding it steady. The square center block is next in order

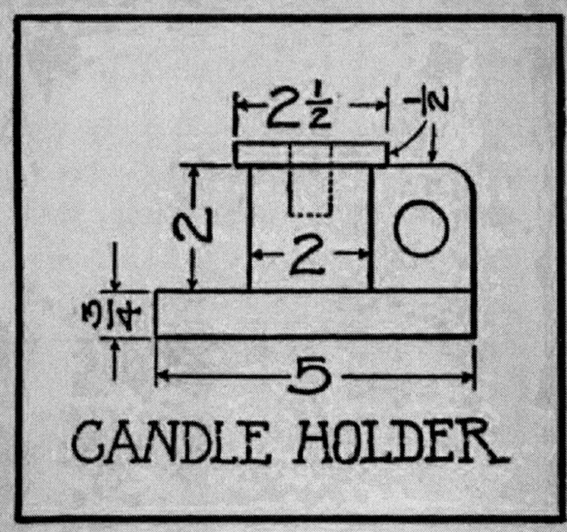

CANDLE HOLDER

and in sawing this out be sure to get it perfectly square and flat on the ends or there will be seams at the top and bottom when the other pieces are put on. Bore a hole in the center the size of a candle and three-quarters of an inch deep and then fasten the block in the exact center of the base board and square with the sides by nailing up through the bottom. The top piece is now to be marked out and the exact center found by drawing diagonal lines from corner to corner. Before cutting this piece out it would be best to bore the central hole for the candle, because the larger the piece of wood the less apt is it to split. This also applies to the hole in the small piece that forms the handle. The top and handle may be fastened on with some small brads, but a neater job will result if we use a little glue instead of the nails. Paint the top of the center block with glue and let this thoroughly dry. Then apply another coat and also coat the under side of the top block, which should then be put in place and some heavy weights placed on it overnight. The handle may then be fitted in and fastened in the same way.

The candle-stick is made in a similar manner. The base consists of a small block on top of a larger one with a very small block on the bottom at each corner. The long center piece should first be smoothed up perfectly square, after which the corners should be cut away as indicated in the drawing, and a hole the size of a candle bored in the center of the top to depth of about three-quarters of an inch. These pieces may all be nailed together without any of the nails show-

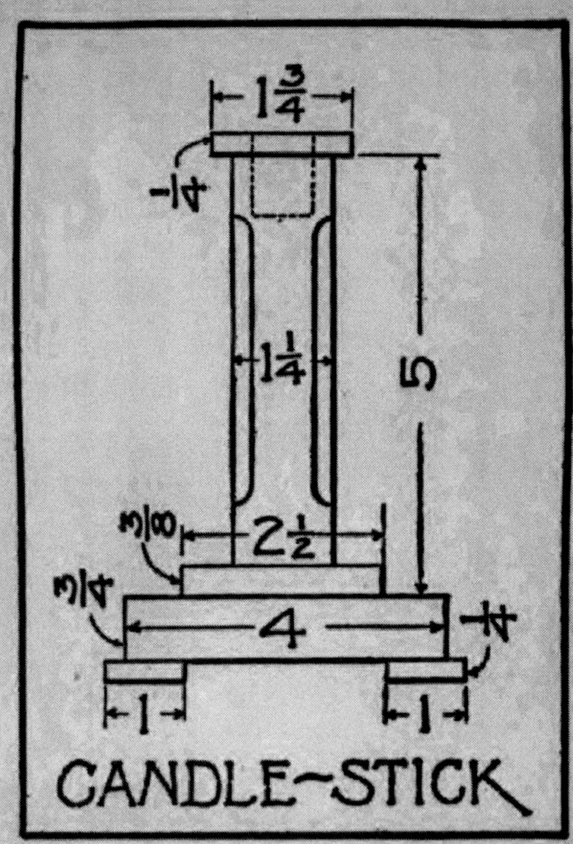

CANDLE-STICK

ing, but the small top block should be glued on as we did before. As you sand-paper the edges of the different pieces smooth, test them often with the square to make sure that you are not rubbing one side down more than another. This applies particularly to the bottom end of the long center piece, which must stand perfectly straight.

The pieces should be stained to match the furniture of the room where they are to be used and rubbed with wax, as previously described.

We now present a pair of candlesticks of more

elaborate construction and intended to be provided with ornamental shades, which may be had in many attractive forms at the department stores at a very reasonable cost. Those who wish to make their own shades from cardboard and colored papers will find instructions for laying them out at the conclusion of this subject.

The construction of the candlestick at the left should start with the base, which, after having been trimmed up perfectly square and sharp on the edges, is to receive a square mortise in the center to hold the lower end of the post. Then cut the post to length and tenon it to match the base, after which accurately mark off the fluting in the sides with a sharp pencil. A sharp gouge will be necessary in working on these half-round grooves. Work from both ends toward the middle, and slowly. Now build out the top by the addition of four small pieces, which are fitted together at the corners with miter joints. Attach with glue, and clamp firmly until dry. The four small foot blocks, and the block on top of the base are now in order. In making the latter be careful not to split it while mortising. Now attach these five pieces with glue and small wire nails. The hole in the top of the post for the candle is now in order, after which the post may be fitted into the base and made secure with glue and a couple of nails driven in from below.

In constructing the base of the candlestick at the right some little care will be necessary in working the base block into the pyramid form. First square it up accurately and then draw all the necessary guide lines, after which take a fine saw and remove two sides opposite to one another. Finish these down to line before starting the other two sides.

Mortise a square hole in the center and finish

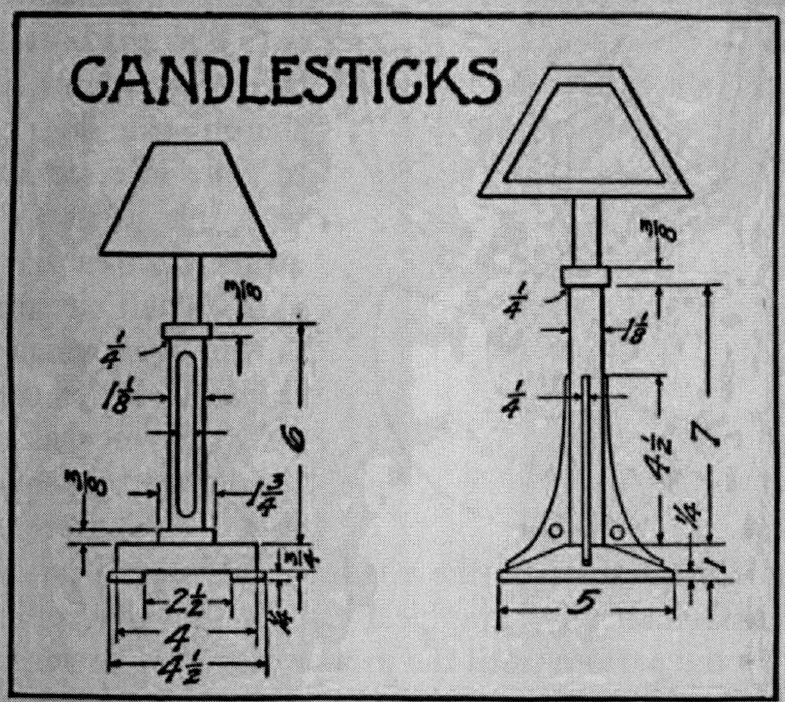

with sandpaper. Prepare the center post as in the previous case except that the sides are left plain. Make ready the four curved brackets, and in finishing their edges work up all four together so as to avoid rounding. Now fit together the whole, and after marking off the position of the brackets on the post and base, set up permanently with glue. Clamp tightly until the glue sets.

To lay out conical shade: Given the top and bottom diameters and the height, make a paper pattern: on a large sheet of paper draw out the shade and then continue the slanting side lines up to an intersection; with this point as a center draw a large and a small circle as shown, after which it only remains to step off a distance along the larger arc equal to the circumference of the bottom of the shade. This may be done mathematically, graphically, or simply by rolling up the pattern until the proper diameter is secured.

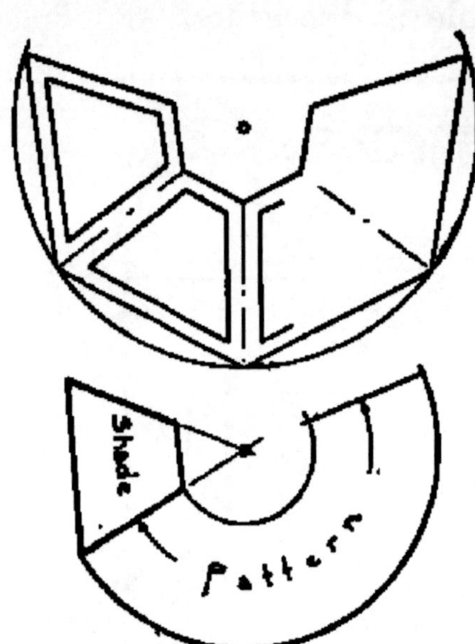

In the construction of the square tapering shade use a cardboard frame and fill in the four panels with either plain or figured tissue. To make a cardboard frame first lay out a pattern of one of the sides, and cut it out so that it can be marked off on the cardboard. Repeat this operation four times, using rather thin, tough cardboard. The first and last sections may be joined by passe-partout tape, after which the top is filled in with a square piece having a round hole in the center just large enough to fit over the shade holder.

MATCH BOX

A match box, a place to strike a light, and a calendar all in one—a practical and interesting problem for any boy or girl carpenter. One can always find a neat calendar pad, which is easily pasted in place, and a piece of emery-cloth or sandpaper makes the finest sort of a place to scratch a light. Either may be renewed as often as necessary.

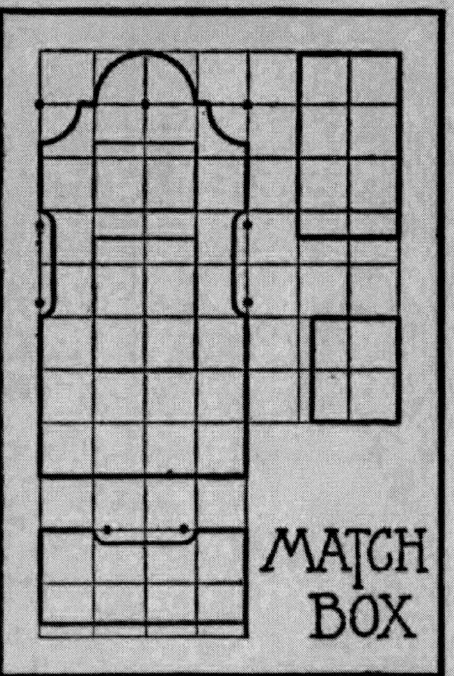

The woodwork is simple. First get a smooth flat board about three-eighths of an inch thick, four inches wide, and eight inches long. Mark this out lightly in one-inch squares, and then with the sharp point of the compasses set on the points marked with the black dots on the drawing, draw the necessary curves. Next join these up with pencil and ruler, and then carefully proceed to saw away the unnecessary wood. Do not saw quite down to the pencil marks, as a small margin must be left for trimming the edges smooth with knife and sandpaper. Apply the try-square every now and then to make sure you are not cutting the edges off on the slant. If you can find some round article of a size that will just fit

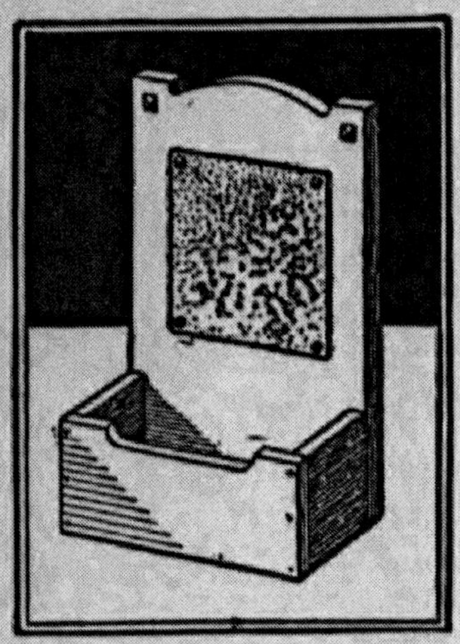

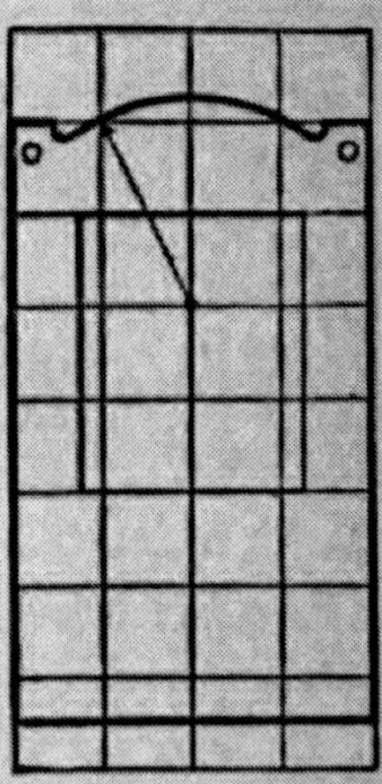

into the curves and wrap it with a piece of sandpaper, the curved edges can be finished much more neatly.

The lower portion of the box is made of thinner wood—about one-quarter inch stuff. First make the front piece and then the ends. Nail these together and to the back board, and then fit in the bottom.

If a calendar is not desired, the size of the back may be cut down a little as shown in the second match box, but the lower part will be the same in both.

The wood should be stained, waxed and well-rubbed. The emery-cloth or sandpaper for striking the light may be pasted on or tacked in place with brass-headed nails. Cut the piece squarely and round the corners slightly. Do not use a good pair of scissors or your best knife for cutting emery- or sandpaper, as it will take the edge off.

TOOTH-BRUSH RACK

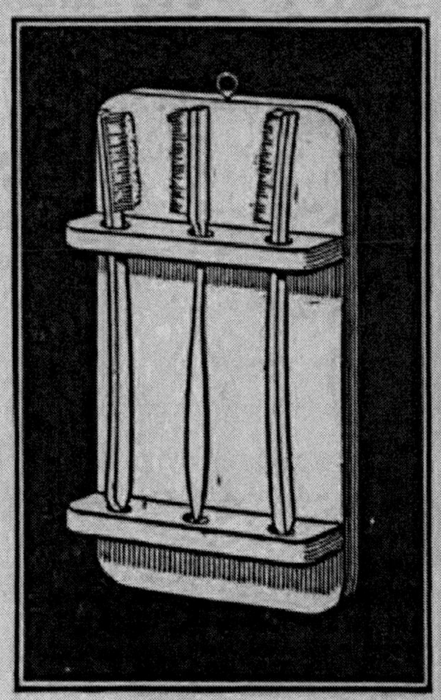

Tooth-brushes look so much alike that it is really very necessary to have a separate place for each brush, and as it is not sanitary to have the damp bristles rubbing around on some dusty surface, we should either hang the brushes up or stand them on end. As most brushes have no holes in the end, the best plan is to make the little rack illustrated, which makes a very neat addition to the bathroom when it is white enameled. This enamel comes in small cans and is applied with a brush just like paint. While one coat will do, a much nicer

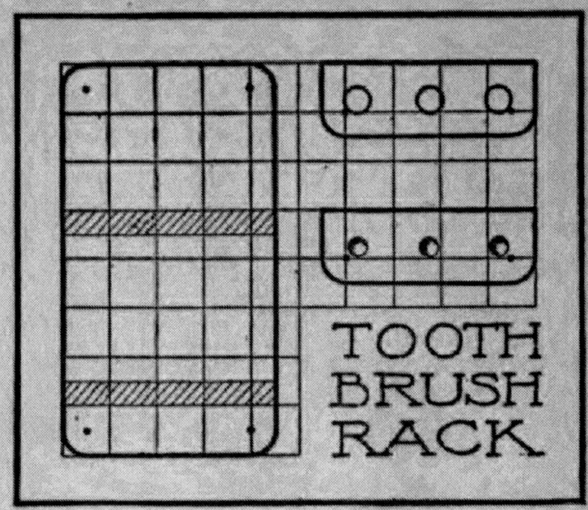

finish will result if the first coat is lightly rubbed with very fine sandpaper and a second one added. Be sure that the first is not only dry but hard before rubbing.

The woodwork is very simple. The pieces should be three-eighths or one-half inch thick, and the proper sizes can easily be determined from the working drawing by counting the number of one-inch squares. The only difficulty you may have will be in boring the three holes in the top piece without splitting. This can be avoided by boring the holes in a piece several inches too long and then cutting off the ends to the proper length. As soon as the point of the bit comes through, turn the wood over and bore from the other side, so as not to make any splinters. Sandpaper the insides and edges of the holes perfectly smooth. In the bottom piece three hollow spots must be gouged out to keep the lower ends of the brushes from slipping around. Set the points of the compasses one-half inch apart and mark the corners for rounding. Attach the top and bottom pieces to the back by nailing in from behind, and after the enameling is done place a screw eye in the top for hanging.

WHISK BROOM HOLDER

The little whisk broom holder which we are now going to construct makes a very neat and practical present. We feel quite sure that any boy or girl who presents this to his or her mother—after it is all stained and waxed, with a neat little calendar pad in place—is pretty sure to be repaid with some nice new tools.

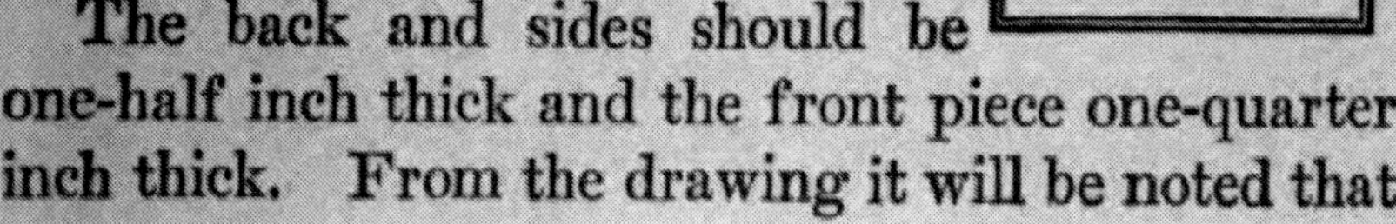

The back and sides should be one-half inch thick and the front piece one-quarter inch thick. From the drawing it will be noted that the back board is five by nine. Square up the ends and mark out the outline very lightly with a sharp pencil, remembering that it is not necessary to cover the entire board with squares as in the drawing. Use the compasses to get the proper curves, and when these are sawn out with the fret saw,

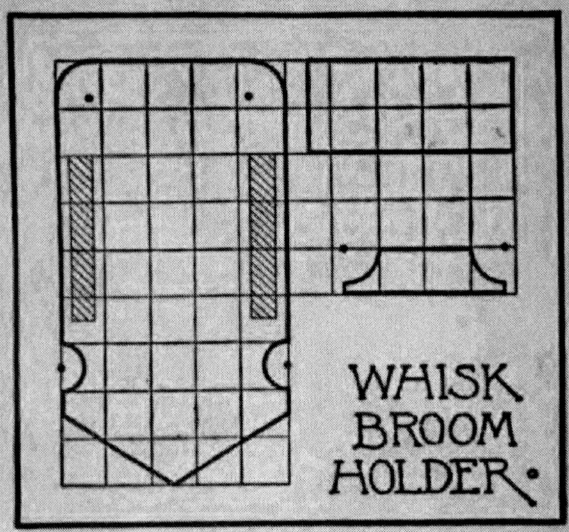

rub the edges smooth with a piece of sandpaper wrapped on something round that will fit the curves. Before nailing up, hold the pieces together and put in the broom to make sure that it will fit. If it is very large or very small, some change may be necessary. Fasten the sides on by small brads driven in from behind, and while the front may also be nailed on, a neater appearance will result if it is fastened with glue and put under a heavy weight all night. Bore a hole near the top so that it may be hung up and then stain and rub with wax, after which paste on the calendar pad.

PIPE RACK

In the making of this pipe rack there is room for the young carpenter to exercise considerable ingenuity, particularly in arranging the decoration in the center. If a nice shiny picture tile can be found, the wood should be hollowed out and the tile set in, or, if it is not too thick, it may be held on the outside by means of small strips fastened around like a frame. If a tile cannot be found, a picture printed on card or heavy paper will answer, but this must not be put on until after the staining and waxing is done. When the time comes, use a little glue and pile on heavy books to keep it from wrinkling.

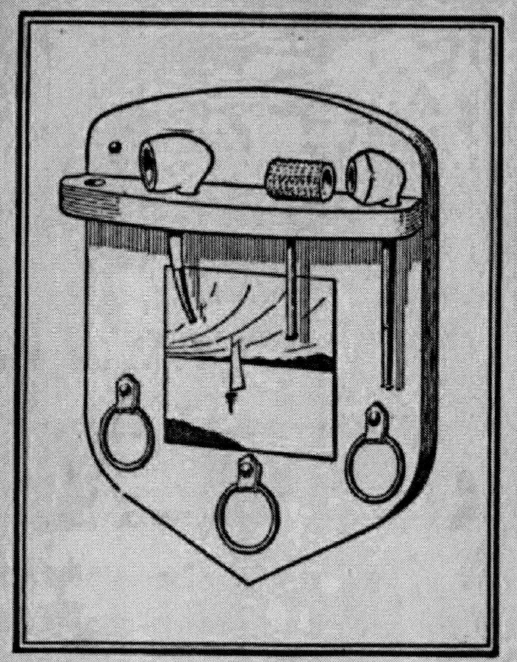

The wood should be three-quarters of an inch thick. The pattern may be marked out directly on the board or upon a smooth flat sheet of paper.

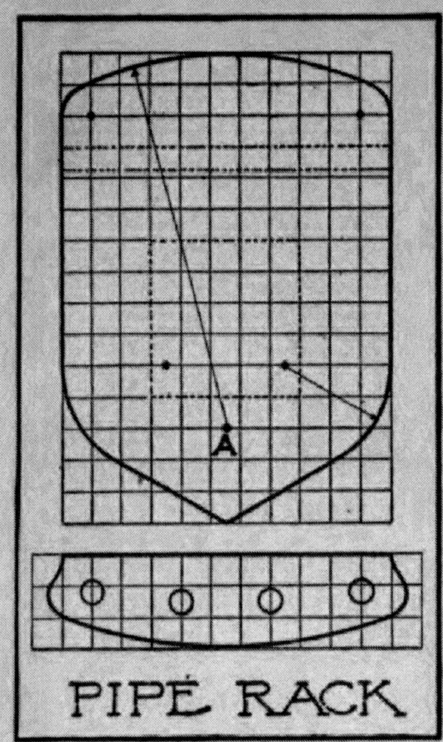

After studying the drawing it will be noted that the outline is controlled by parts of circles drawn from the five center points indicated by the black dots. When these circles are drawn, no difficulty will be found in completing the outline with pencil and ruler. As the compasses will not be large enough to draw the top curve, drive in a pin at the point A and use a piece of string looped around the pencil. Saw away the extra wood, cutting almost to the line, then trim with the knife and plane, finishing with sandpaper on a block. In order to get the edge flat all the way round, test it every little while with the square, otherwise you are sure to spoil the outline.

The pattern for the shelf piece may be readily sketched out on paper if three rows of one-inch squares are first drawn. The pencil and string will again be found useful in drawing the long curve. Bore the holes before trimming the edges off, and as soon as the point of the bit is felt coming through, take it out and bore from the other side, so as not to tear off splinters. Sandpaper the insides and the edges of the holes smooth and then fasten the shelf in place with nails driven in from behind.

The three large rings may be used for more pipes or else for neckties. If the rings cannot be found around the house, the harness store can supply them, and also the small strips of leather to attach them, all of which should be done after staining and waxing.

SALT BOX

It is always advisable to stand well with the cook, and one sure way of accomplishing this is to make the neat little salt box illustrated, and hang it up in the kitchen at the most convenient point.

The wood should be about three-eighths of an inch thick and cut according to the working drawing, in which each small square represents exactly one inch. First make the back and then the sides. Fasten these together by nailing from behind. Next fit in the front and then the bottom, which goes clear inside of the other pieces. When these are all nailed up, the lid should be fitted so as to

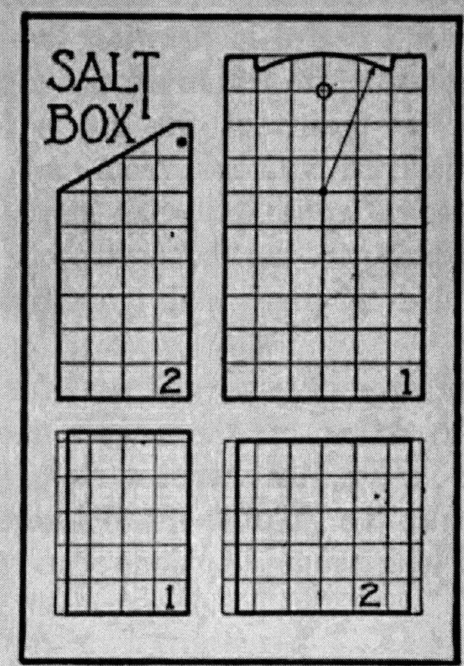

lift up and down easily without binding or leaving gaping seams at the sides. After rounding the back edge of the lid, set it in place and very carefully drive in a small nail through each side at the top corner into the lid so as to serve as a hinge. The place for these nails is indicated by the black spot on the pattern for the side, but do not drive the nails clear in until you have tried the lid to see that it raises up properly, and have also applied the necessary finish.

This box may be white enameled or shellacked over the natural wood without staining.

TOWEL-ROLLER

Do not start to make a towel-roller until you have found a piece of round wood, such as a curtain pole, suitable for the roller. All the old paint and varnish should be removed and the surface sandpapered fresh and clean. The back piece should be about a half inch

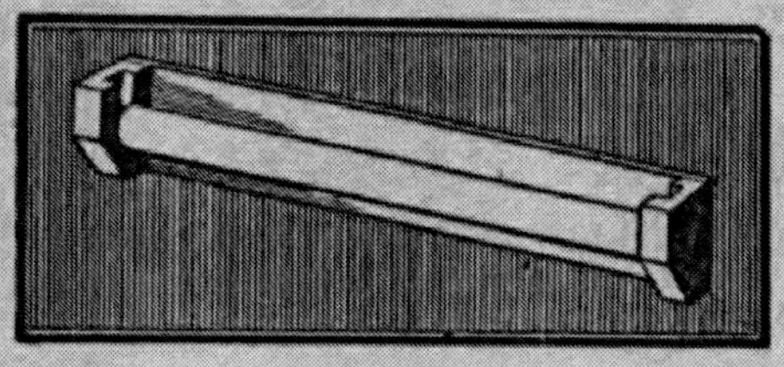

thick and twenty inches long, although this measurement may have to be changed a little if the toweling is of some special width. The shape of the end blocks is clearly shown in the drawing. A hole about a half or three-quarters of an inch in diameter is to be bored in the center half-way through, after which the wood extending from the hole to the top of the block is to be cut away, so that the roller may be slipped in. Saw off

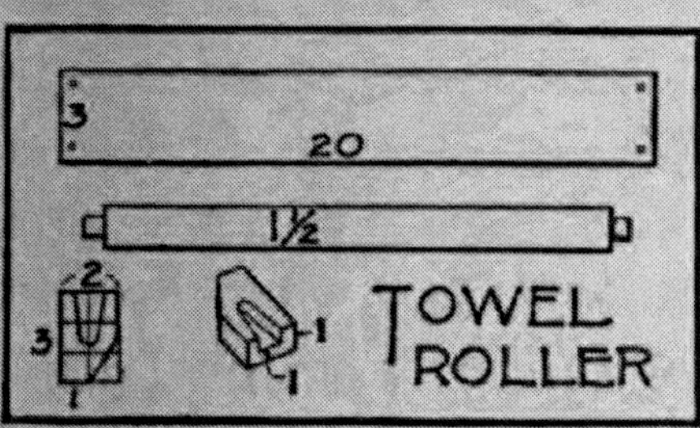

the lower front corner of each block and attach by driving nails in through the back. The ends of the roller are now to be worked down evenly all the way round, so that it will run freely between the end blocks.

The finish may be white enamel or shellac varnish on the natural wood, depending on the woodwork in the room where it is to be used.

SLEEVE-BOARD

Ironing shirtwaists and pressing suits is hard work at best, and, as every girl and boy wishes to have their clothes look neat, the least that the young carpenter can do is to get out the tools and make a

neat little sleeve-board so that every convenience may be at hand.

Before starting the actual construction, consult with mother or sister and see whether the thirty-inch board shown in the drawing would be the most convenient size. Should some slight change be found necessary in the top, it is not likely that the lower part need be changed, but even should one wish to change it all around, no difficulty will be found as the small squares indicate the proper proportions.

The top and bottom pieces are two one-inch boards, which measure seven-eighths after being planed at the mill. Be sure that the pieces selected have no knots, or the resin will come out with the heat. Draw a five-inch circle at one end of the top

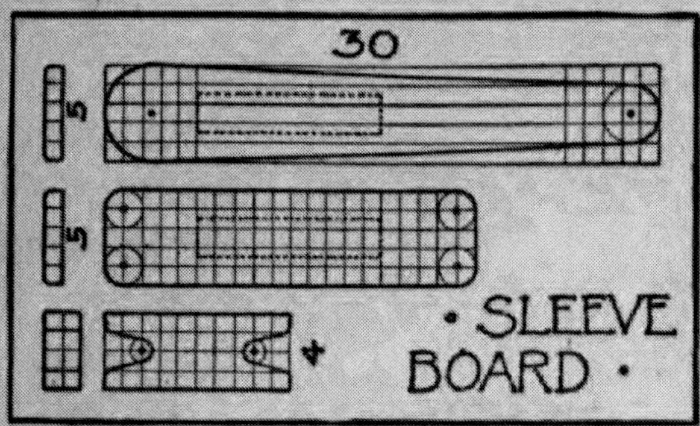

board and a three-inch one at the other, and then join these by two straight lines. Saw and plane off the sides, and then saw the ends round with the keyhole saw, finishing them smooth with sandpaper. Next square up the base board and draw a two-inch circle at each corner, which should then be rounded off accordingly. It now remains to prepare the center piece, which is to be two inches thick. Bore two one-inch holes clear through at the points marked in the working drawing, after which saw out the V-shaped piece at each end and round the corners, so that they will not catch whatever is being pressed. Fasten this piece in place by driving nails in through the bottom, and then nail on the top. In order to have these pieces properly centered, mark out the position of the center piece on both the top and bottom. All corners should be well rounded and sandpapered smooth.

STATIONERY RACK

A stationery rack is something that may be made in a very short time, but if it is made as it should be, with the outline sharp and true and the seams all closely fitted, it will require a lot of care and attention.

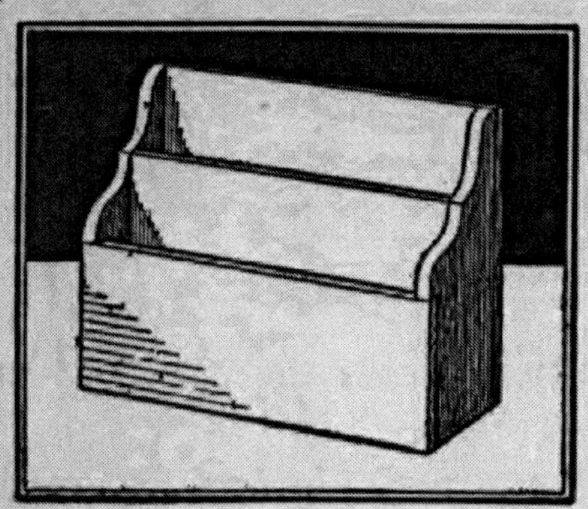

The size will depend somewhat on the size of the stationery one uses, but any slight change in the width and height need not affect the depth from front to back or the curved outline.

On the end pieces mark out some one-inch squares, using the steel square to see that they are true. Set the points of the compasses exactly one inch apart and then with the pointed end on each of the four center points marked by the black dots in the working drawing, draw four quarter circles, and you will immediately have the proper shape for the ends. Before sawing these out with the fret saw, cut out a strip along the front of each end board just wide enough to let the front piece set in. Place the two ends together and sandpaper the edges flat and smooth. For the curves wrap the sand paper around something round, such as a can about two inches in diameter. The front and back pieces are plain boards, sawn off perfectly square on the ends. If you have any trouble in keeping the edges from becoming rounded while sandpapering them, nail the front and back to the ends so that they will project beyond just a trifle, and then after the bottom is fitted

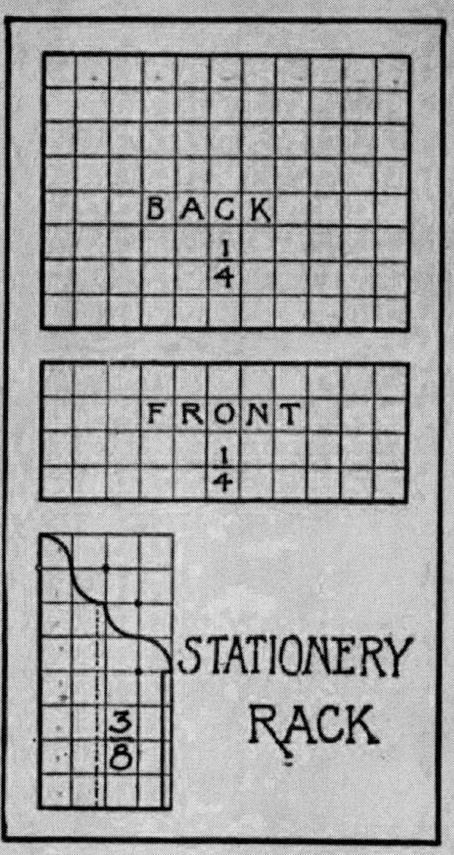

in you may sandpaper them off exactly even with the end boards. The center board now remains to be closely fitted in place, but before nailing this in, it and the rest of the rack should be stained the desired shade and rubbed with wax, as it would be very inconvenient to get at the inside after the center piece is in place. The heads of the small brads used in the construction should be well set into the wood and puttied over.

If you happen to have some large clamps and good glue, the front piece may be put on without nails. If you try this have everything ready before putting on the glue.

BATHROOM MIRROR

A combination of a towel-roller and a mirror is now presented. Before proceeding with it, first procure the mirror itself. While the dimensions given are quite usual, yet there is no absolute standard among the makers. It would also be well to give some consideration to the towel supply and the required width, after which it is a very simple matter to determine the remaining dimensions of this convenient article.

The first object will be to make the rectangular frame with mortise connections, and then corner

BATHROOM MIRROR

out the back edges around the opening to hold the glass. The vertical pieces, it will be noted, extend downward to hold the shelf-brackets, which may now be made ready. If a roller-towel is to be used, one bracket must have a hole clear through, so that the roller may be withdrawn. It then remains only to make the shelf and assemble the parts. Glue the mortises; fasten the other pieces with screws from behind, and glue.

MILL BILL

PCS.	DIMENSIONS
2	⅞ x 3¼ x 20
2	⅞ x 3¼ x 16
1	¾ x 3¾ x 22
2	¾ x 3¼ x 5

STATIONERY CABINET

The little stationery-cabinet would delight a small sister or brother of school age, and be very useful to many an older person. For any one who has no desk it would be most convenient, as a neat little stationery-cabinet practically transforms a table into a desk. Ink, pens, pencils, stamps, wax, and the seal may all be placed in the little drawer, and two sizes of stationery, envelopes, and correspondence may all be disposed of in the space above. Before adopting the dimensions given, consider them carefully in relation to your own special requirements, and any changes desired should be worked out full size on a sheet of paper. Then again, the thickness of the wood is subject to great variation, and may be reduced quite a little if the home carpenter feels competent to handle it.

Those who can plane narrow slots across the two end boards to hold the ends of the top, bottom, and shelves, may make all connections merely with glue; others will have to supplement the glue with some

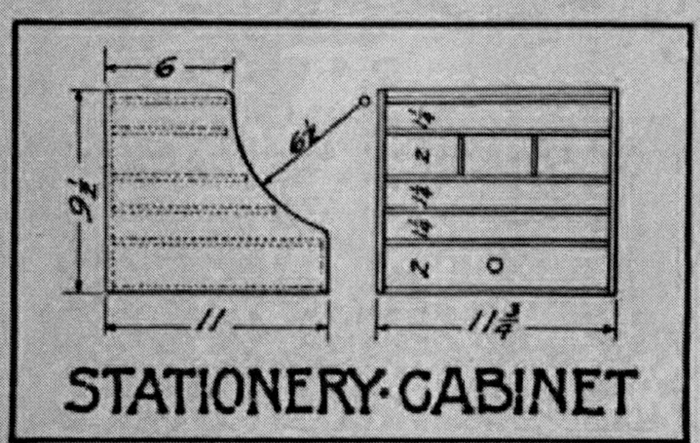

STATIONERY · CABINET

small brads. The entire structure should be assembled before making the drawer, which, with the exception of the front, should be made from as thin material as possible.

Mill Bill

PCS.	DIMENSIONS
2	⅜ x 11½ x 10
2	¼ x 6 x 11½
1	¼ x 7 x 11½
1	¼ x 8¼ x 11½
2	¼ x 11 x 11½
1	¼ x 9¾ x 12

STATIONERY RACK AND INKSTAND

Just think—a stationery rack, inkstand, pen and pencil holder, and calendar all in one, which any boy or girl may make for a few cents. Besides the wood, all that is needed is a small glass ink pot, such as is used in school desks.

There are but five pieces of wood and these are only one-quarter of an inch thick. First mark out the sides very carefully. Make the curves with

the compasses and then cut the wood exactly to line. The upright pieces are set into slots cut in the sides, so be sure that these slots are just large enough to make a tight fit. After the two sides are cut to line, place them together, sandpaper the edges flat and smooth, and hollow out the places for the pen and pencil. The two upright pieces require no attention aside from having their ends made smooth and the corners rounded. The last of the five pieces is for the ink pot, and should have a hole bored or sawn in the center just large enough to hold it firmly. Fasten each side to this piece with two nails and then set the uprights in place, applying a little glue in the slots already cut in the side pieces. Before allowing these to set, however, be sure that the sides are perfectly parallel and stand straight. It now only remains to find something round for a cover for the ink pot. If a suitable cover cannot be found, simply cut out a neat disc of thin wood and fasten a small knob on top in the center.

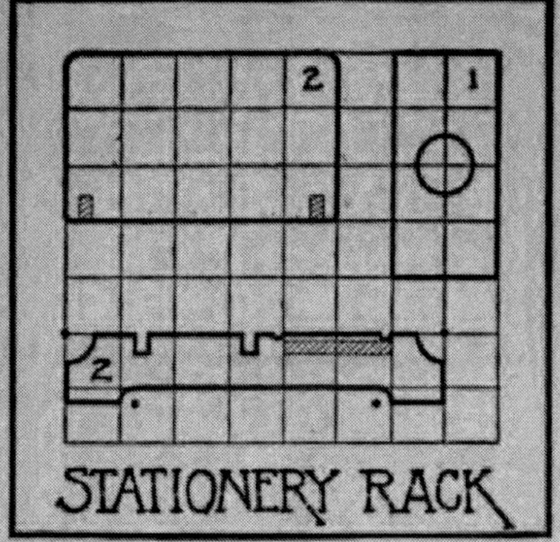

STATIONERY RACK

It will often be found more convenient to stain and wax the different pieces after they are all perfectly fitted, but before nailing them together. When the article is completed all finger marks should then be removed by going over the surface again with the waxy rag.

BOOK-RACKS

While we are furnishing up our desk it would be well to consider the question of a book-rack for it. The rack illustrated is large enough to hold all of

your study books or may be used to hold the current books being read by the rest of the family.

The end boards should be three-quarters of an inch thick and carefully marked out, as shown in the working drawing. If the sharp point of the compasses is placed exactly at the center points indicated by the black dots, no difficulty will be found in getting the curves. The only trouble will be in cutting the edge of the board exactly true with your lines. Do not saw too close, and when trimming off, frequently test with the try-square, or you will be almost sure to cut away too much on one side. When both ends are finally worked down to line, place them back to back, with penciled sides out, and sandpaper the edges until they are exactly alike.

The two side boards should be about five-eighths of an inch thick and require only to be sawn off perfectly square on the ends and exactly the same length. Mark the places where these go on the end pieces and then nail the whole together. If you happen to know how to use dowel pins, the pieces

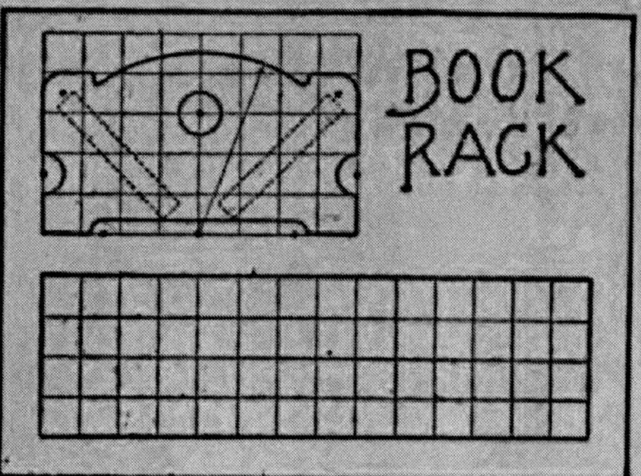

may be fastened without nails. Dowels are simply short pieces of round wood. When a connection is to be made in this manner a hole just large enough to let the pin fit in tightly is bored in each of the two pieces *exactly* opposite. The pin is then coated with glue and driven into one of the holes. When the glue has set the other pieces may be temporarily driven on, and if everything fits together properly the pieces are taken apart and some glue applied to the other half of the pin, after which they are put together again for good. Usually not less than two dowel pins are used for each connection.

Stain, and if nails are used, putty over the heads with stained putty and rub with wax—all as previously described.

The second book-rack is made entirely of three-quarter-inch square strips. Should you desire to increase the extent, the size of the material used will have to be increased. When it is explained that all connections in this piece are "cross-lapped," that is, each piece is reduced to one-half its thickness at the point of crossing, little more need be said as to the construction.

First cut the several pieces to the proper lengths and then point up the ends, taking due care that all

pieces are perfectly square and of the same size. With all possible accuracy mark off with a sharp pencil the various places to be cut out. Work up each end, putting the pieces together with glue and clamping tightly. Finally connect the two ends with the side pieces. The four feet should each be covered with felt.

MILL BILL

PCS.	DIMENSIONS
2	¾ x ¾ x 18½
4	¾ x ¾ x 7½
2	¾ x ¾ x 8½
2	¾ x ¾ x 8

PUTTING UP A SHELF

Almost every one knows how to put up the ordinary shelf—simply screw two brackets to the wall

and a board on top, and the job is done. But supposing there is no room for brackets, as, for example, is usually the case over the kitchen sink,—what then? Just turn the brackets upside down and "hang" the shelf in place. If the place where the top screws are to be put, stands out from the wall, set the brackets a little forward on the shelf board so that the back edge will naturally hang against the wall and you will find this sort of a shelf very safe and steady.

A much more interesting task, however, is to

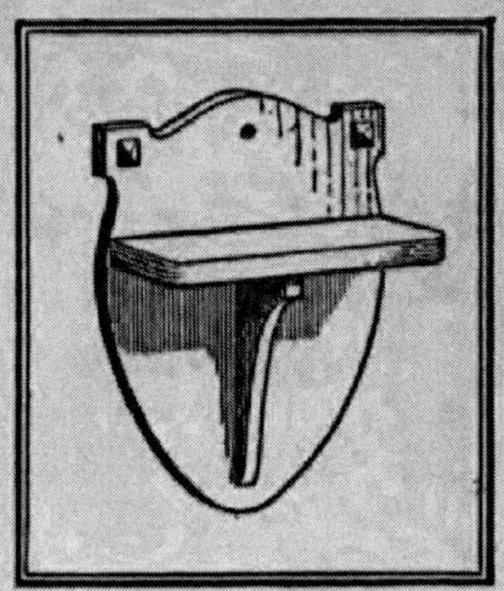

make the small clock bracket illustrated. The laying out of the sides is in itself an interesting lesson in curves. By examining the working drawing we find the back is eight by ten inches. Get a smooth flat board not less than one-half inch thick and lightly mark out the one-inch squares with a sharp pencil. Examine the drawing again and you will notice that there are two side curves, a top curve and one for the bottom. Each curve has its own center, the position of which is clearly indicated in the drawing by a black dot. Place the sharp point of the compasses on each of these dots and spread the pencil point until it touches the outside line at the top, bottom or side of the board, as the case may be. With these curves drawn, the rest of the outline may be finished in a few minutes.

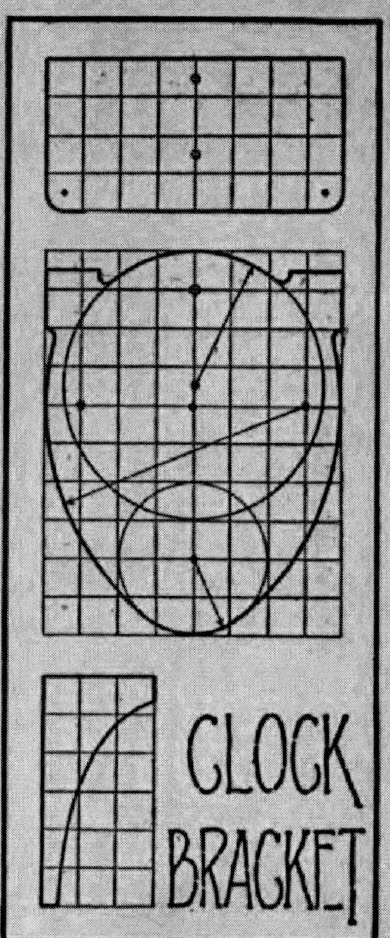

The curve of the small piece under the shelf board is not part of a circle and must be sketched in freehand after the small squares are drawn as a guide. The shelf board requires no special attention after the ends are made perfectly smooth and square, except to have its corners rounded. Fasten this to the back board by means of nails driven in from behind, and then attach the bracket piece in the same manner, after which drive in two nails down through the shelf.

The bracket may be hung upon the wall by a nail

in the center, or better still, by one at each corner. In this case the holes should be about a quarter of an inch in diameter, and in order to hide the heads of the two nails set in the wall, shape up two three-quarter inch squares of wood about one-quarter of an inch thick, and then whittle them to a dull point, as illustrated. By gluing one of these on at each of the upper corners, the supporting nails will be completely hidden.

FLOWER BRACKET

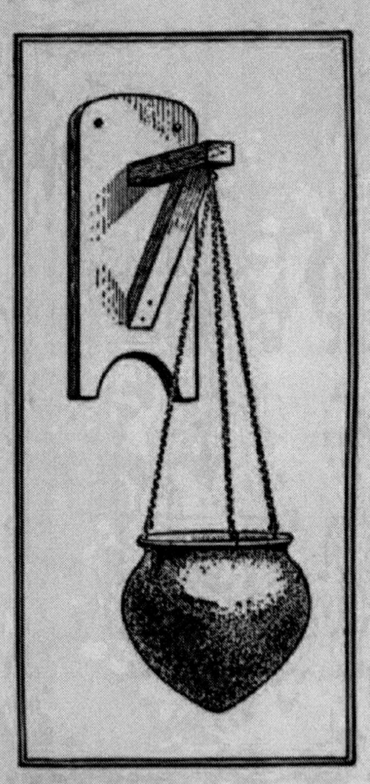

The department stores nowadays sell so many beautiful brass and pottery flower jars at a very low price that there is no excuse for any house not having a lovely hanging fern, provided there is a young carpenter at hand to make a nicely stained and waxed bracket from which to suspend it. From our drawing it will be noted that a suitable bracket is not hard to make, as only three pieces of wood are used.

The back board is four by

nine inches and should be about one-half inch thick. Three separate curves enter into the form of the top line, but these may be very quickly drawn with the compasses if you make sure they are centered exactly on the points marked with the black dots in the working drawing. Saw away the extra material with the fret saw, and finish the edges smooth with plane and sandpaper. Plane up a strip long enough to make the two pieces that project out, sawing off the one perfectly square and the other at forty-five degrees, which is the angle made by folding a square of paper in two from opposite corners. Fasten the upper one in place by nailing in through the back and then nail on the slanting brace, which operation will require a little care in order to keep from bending the top piece out of place.

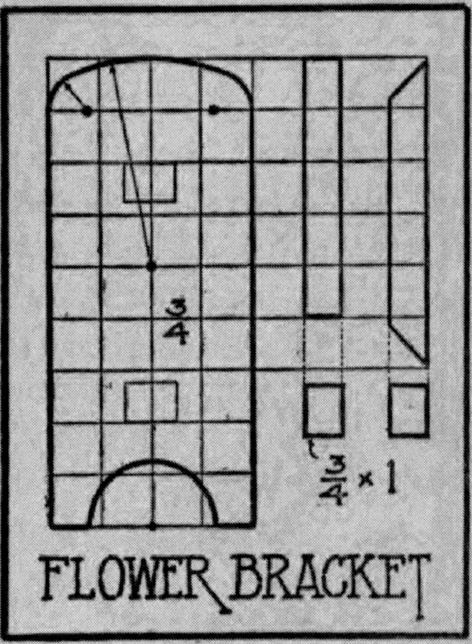

FLOWER BRACKET

This bracket will be found large enough for almost any ordinary flower jar. Sometimes, however, long, narrow, pointed jars are used, in which case a more slender bracket would be appropriate. When a change, such as this, appears desirable, always mark out the lines of the new piece full size on a sheet of paper in order to be sure that it will look well.

FOOTSTOOL

A footstool is always a handy article to have around, and one with a place for the hand, so that it may be readily carried about, is especially useful in the kitchen. Haven't you noticed how the cook likes to hold the pan in her lap when shelling peas or cleaning strawberries?—and how often the shelf in the pantry is just a few inches too high! Our drawing shows how to make a footstool out of five pieces only.

The material should be seven-eighths of an inch thick, which is the thickness of one-inch boards after the mill gets through planing them. First trim off the ends perfectly square and then saw out the feet with the fret or keyhole saw. Saw out each of the upper corners just enough to allow the side pieces to fit in evenly with the edges. The side pieces are now to be marked out in accordance with the drawing and their edges worked down smoothly and square with the sides, after which only the top remains. Saw the ends of this piece off squarely, round the corners, and then with the plane round off the top edge all the way around. To form the opening for the hand, bore two holes

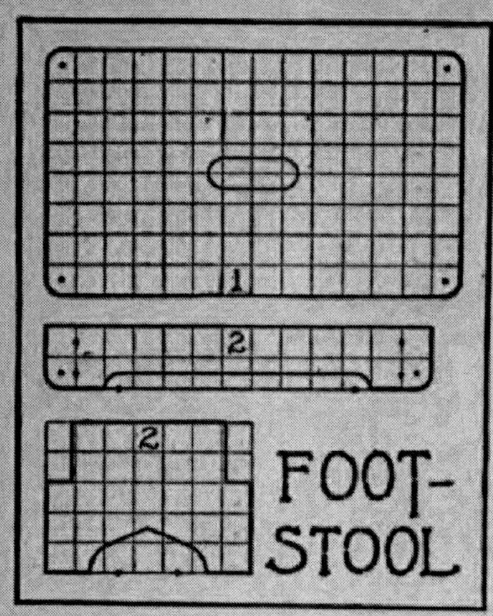

and saw out the wood in between, after which the edges should be worked smooth with sandpaper. Nail the sides to the two ends, and then fasten on the top. This may be done by nailing in through the top, or more neatly by screws put in from underneath from the inside at an angle.

BLACKING STAND

Blacking one's shoes is no trouble at all when by merely lifting a lid you can find everything right at hand—brushes, polish and all—including a block to keep your foot from slipping. This is exactly what the blacking stand illustrated provides.

The working drawing clearly shows the method of laying out the end boards. These and all of the other pieces are made of inch lumber after it has been dressed smooth. On the center line of each end mark a point five inches from the bottom, and, with the sharp point of the compasses placed there draw a six-inch circle, after which draw a line from each side of this circle down to a point on the bottom line an inch and a half from the outside corner. Saw out the piece in between, using the regular saw on the straight part and the keyhole saw on the curves. Finish the edges smooth and saw out a strip at each side near the top so that the side pieces will fit in. The other pieces are of the sizes noted in the drawing and require nothing further than trimming up true and square with smooth flat ends.

In putting together, first nail the sides to the

ends, and then fit in the bottom, nailing it in place through the sides and ends. Next nail on one-half of the top, and then hinge the other half to it, after which it only requires the addition of the foot block to complete the stand ready for staining.

The most desirable hinges for this purpose are the kind know as *butt* hinges. A pair of these will be necessary, and the width should be about equal to the thickness of the top boards. In order that there will not be a space between the two halves of the top, the wood should be cut away, so as to let the hinges fit in even.

SHOE-BRUSH BOX

Sometimes there is no convenient place to keep a blacking box, in which case the best we can do is to make a shoe-brush box and hang it on the wall. The back space will hold a pair of brushes, and the smaller one in front is for the polish, the daubing brush and polishing rag. The construction is not difficult, and when the box is stained a dark brown or painted black it presents a neat appearance.

The two side pieces should be about a half inch thick, and the back, front and center piece about three-eighths. To get a pattern for the sides, mark out four rows of one-inch squares, eight in a row. Take a pair of compasses and with the sharp point set on the black dots marked on the working drawing, draw in the curves, and you will have the correct shape for the end almost at once. This may all be done on a flat sheet of paper, after which the pattern is cut out with the scissors so that it may be transferred to the wood. Another way is to draw the squares directly on the wood in the first place. This is the more accurate way, and if one edge of the wood is planed exactly straight, so that the square will slide along nicely, the small squares may be very quickly and accurately drawn. Always use a sharp pencil, and do not bear down hard. When the outline is complete saw it out with the fret saw, after which the edges are to be trimmed and sandpapered. The two sides should be exactly the same when placed together.

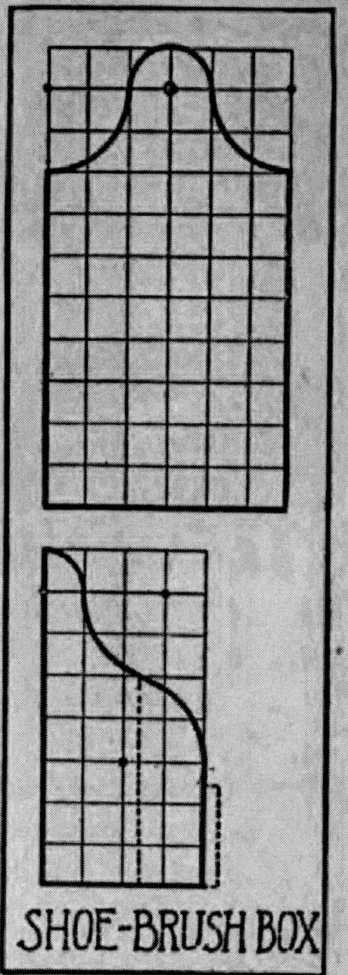
SHOE-BRUSH BOX

The back board is next in order, and should be marked and cut out in the same way as the sides. Bore a quarter-inch hole near the top in the exact center for hanging, after which prepare the front board, which requires no further attention after the ends are trimmed off smooth and square. Be sure that this piece is exactly as long as the back is wide.

The putting together may now begin. Nail through the back into the sides, and then nail on the front, after which the bottom should be cut so that it will fit snugly inside. Nail this in place, and then fit in the center piece, which is fastened in place by nailing in through the sides.

FLOWER STAND

There is nothing that adds so much to the appearance of an indoor plant as to place the pot or jar in which it is growing on an attractive stand. The stand illustrated is very suitable for this, and may also, of course, be used for other purposes.

The construction should commence with the side pieces, which are one-half inch thick. These are all identical, except that two of the four are one inch narrower, so that when the other two are nailed to them the stand will be exactly as wide on one side as another.

On a smooth sheet of paper proceed to mark out the outline in accordance with the working drawing, taking particular care to shape the feet properly. Place the sharp point of the compasses on the small dots, and draw the necessary circles. If these do not cut the small squares exactly as shown, it means that you haven't got the proper center points. In forming the large opening, first draw the seven-inch circle, and then the two smaller curves near the top, after which a piece of string will be necessary for the side curves. The radius of these will be exactly seventeen inches, and the centers are on the same cross line as the center of the seven-inch circle. Simply run this line out to each side, and drive in a tack at the proper point. When the outline is complete, cut out with a sharp knife or very small pair of scissors, and then place it on each of the four side pieces, which should then be marked out

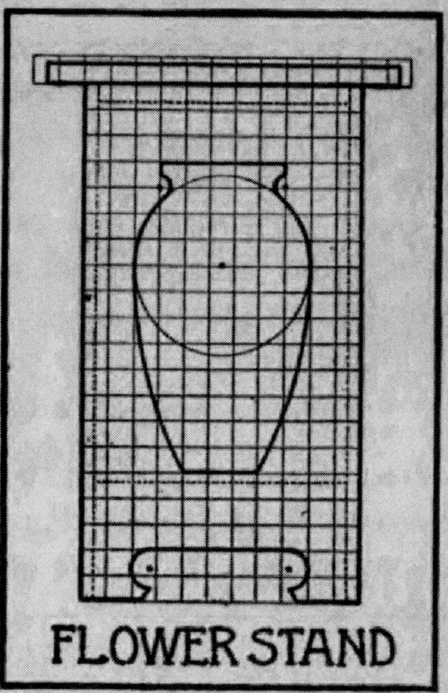
FLOWER STAND

with a sharp pencil. Saw out the large opening, and shape up the feet, all very carefully, so as not to tear off any splinters and thus spoil the outline. Trim off the edges, and smooth with sandpaper, after which the four sides may be nailed together.

A bottom board is now in order, and should be made perfectly square and just large enough to fit snugly inside. The top board, you will note, is to be large enough to project an inch and a half all the way round, and requires no further attention after the ends are worked down with sandpaper on a block until they are smooth and flat. On the under side of this nail a square piece just large enough to fit inside, after which the top may be put in position and fastened down by nailing in through the four sides into this under piece.

Stain as desired, and carefully putty all nail holes, after which a good rubbing with wax will complete the piece.

SLIPPER BOX

The slipper box illustrated is really a box with a door in front, the top being padded so as to make a comfortable leg rest or temporary seat. When father or uncle sits down in the evening in the big chair, his slippers are right at hand, and also a comfortable place to put his feet. At first glance this piece of furniture will appear rather hard to make, but when you learn how to go about it, it is quite simple. Perhaps you may have to get a little assistance when it comes to padding the top, but there surely will be no trouble in that.

All of the pieces should be one-inch dressed lumber. Choose pieces that have a pretty grain and are free from knots. Start with the two ends. Plane up the edges so that the two boards are exactly the proper width, and then lightly mark off the necessary squares with a sharp pencil, using the steel square to keep the lines parallel. Place the sharp point of the compasses on the black dots shown in the working drawing, and draw the necessary curves. The top curve, however, cannot be drawn with the compasses as it is too large. The center point for this is exactly in the middle of the board at the bottom, and the best way is to drive in a tack at this point and use a string. The different curves must now be joined up with pencil and ruler, and when the outline is satisfactorily completed, the sawing out should begin. Saw very

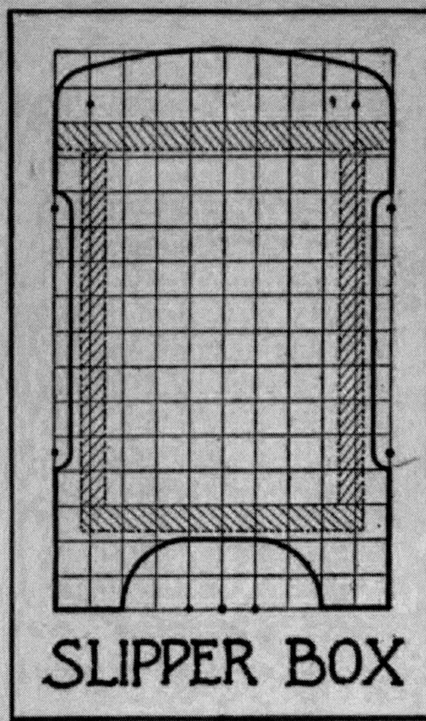

carefully so as not to tear off any splinters, and then take the plane and knife and trim down to line. Test the edges frequently, or you will be sure to trim off more toward one side than toward the other. When the two are finally shaped up, place them together, and sandpaper the edges smooth with a piece of sandpaper wrapped on a block. For the curves, wrap the paper on a round piece of wood.

The top, bottom and back boards are all plain pieces of exactly the same length—all sixteen inches long. The top piece is the same width as the ends, while the bottom is an inch and a half narrower. The width of the back piece is ten and a quarter inches. Before attempting to put together, prepare four square strips, one inch wide and seven inches long. Mark out on the ends exactly where the top and bottom pieces come, and then fasten on these strips to the inside surfaces of the end boards, all as illustrated in the skeleton view. When the strips are securely fastened in place, it is a very simple matter to fasten the top and bottom pieces to them. In all this we may use glue and nails, although a carpenter would probably use screws.

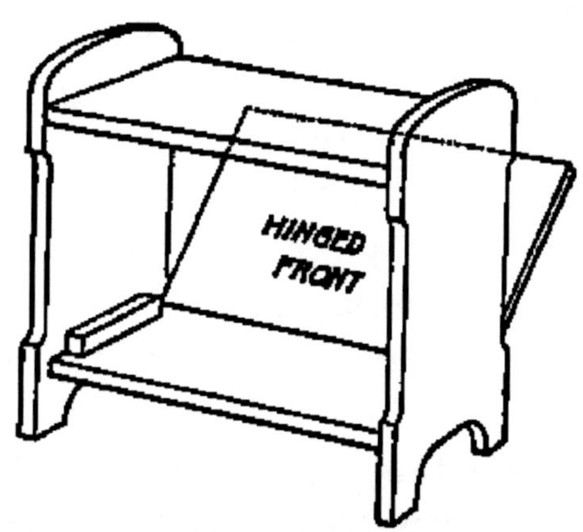

Do not fasten any piece in place until you have fitted them all together to make sure that everything is all right. The back is next to be put in position, and should be just wide enough to fit snugly in between the top and bottom pieces without leaving any seams. It is then fastened in place by nailing in through the top and bottom. The front is the same as the back, except that it is just enough smaller all the way round to permit of it being used as a door. This is to be attached with two hinges at the bottom, and if strap hinges of brass or copper can be obtained at some arts-and-crafts store, they should be used, but if not, simply get the best looking hinges you can at the hardware store. A small knob or cupboard catch to match the hinges should also be purchased and placed in the center near the top of the door.

The staining and waxing are now in order, after which the top is to be upholstered. Go to the furniture store and get sufficient upholstering material to tightly pad the top. Pile this on evenly and draw a piece of cotton or canvas over it, tacking it in place after stretching evenly. With the tape, measure the correct size for the final top covering of imitation leather, allowing enough for turning the edges under. This and about three dozen fancy tacks will complete the job. Tack the leather along one edge of the top board first and then along the other, after which fasten the ends. Be sure the tacks are evenly spaced.

UMBRELLA STAND

As soon as one decides to make an umbrella stand he should be on the outlook for a shallow round pan about six inches in diameter, to place in the bottom to catch the drippings from the wet umbrellas. While a tin pan may be made to answer by enameling it, a brass or copper one will look better and be more durable.

The construction should begin with the two side boards, which should be smooth, free from knots, and about three-eighths of an inch thick. First plane the edges off until each piece is exactly eight inches wide, and then mark out the outline in accordance with the working drawing, in which each square represents one square inch. It will be understood, of course, that it is not necessary to cover the entire board with squares, although enough should be drawn at each end to enable one to readily locate all necessary points. Use the compasses to get the curves, and be sure that the three square openings are all exactly the same size. Saw these out neatly with the fret saw, which should also be used for the circular opening near the top. The long, narrow slot may be worked out with the knife, although sawing will be the safer way. See that all edges and corners are finished sharp and true, and then shape up the top and the two feet at the bottom.

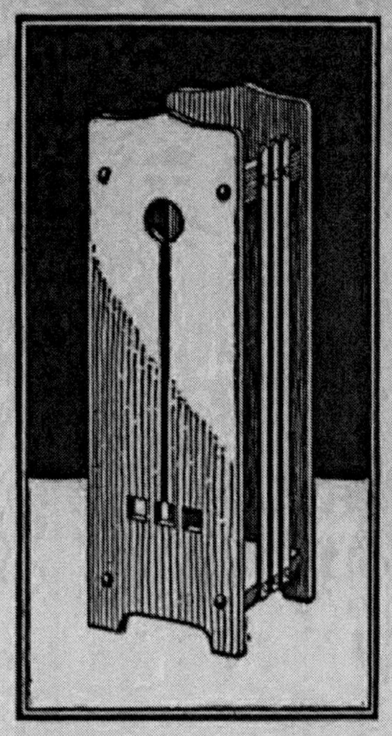

A square board for the bottom is next in order, and a large hole should be sawn in the center of this to let the drip pan set in. The two cross-pieces at the top remain to be prepared and should be exactly as long as the bottom board and perfectly square and flat on the ends. Mark off on the inner surface of each side board just where the other pieces are to be fastened. Fasten one of the sides to the bottom, and then nail on the cross pieces, after which turn over and put on the other side.

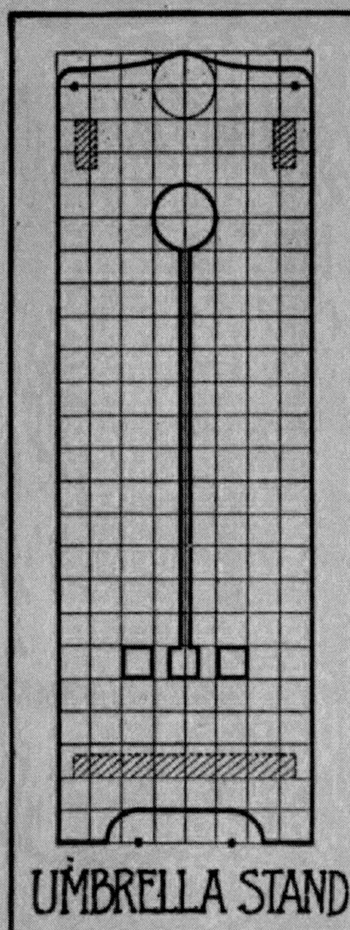
UMBRELLA STAND

Stain to match the surrounding furniture. Apply a coat of thin shellac, rub with steel wool when dry, and then wax. To cover up the nail holes, drive in close to each nail a nail with a large fancy head, or glue on a small round block over each one before staining, taking due care that they are evenly set.

WASTE-BASKET

A waste-basket, when properly made, is one of the most attractive articles that the young carpenter can make for the home. There are six pieces in the basket illustrated, which are laced together near the top with strips of white leather, which is also used to fasten on the two large rings that serve as handles.

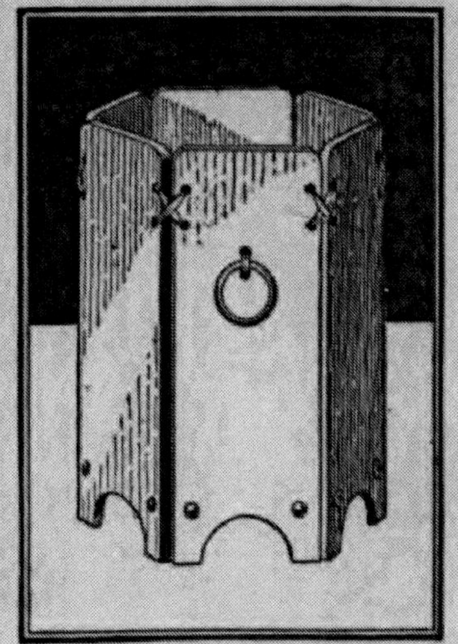

The six side pieces should be from one-quarter to three-eighths of an inch thick. Square them up all exactly the same size, and then use the compasses to draw the half circle at the bottom of each piece and the quarter circle at each of the upper corners. Do not mark one board from another, but use the compasses on each one separately. Six quarter-inch holes must now be bored in each piece as indicated, due care being taken not to tear off any splinters.

The marking out of the bottom is very simple. On a large piece of smooth paper draw a straight line A—C exactly twelve inches long Place the point of the compasses at A and draw a half circle through the center point B. Then place the compasses at C and draw another half circle through B, after which place the point at B and draw a

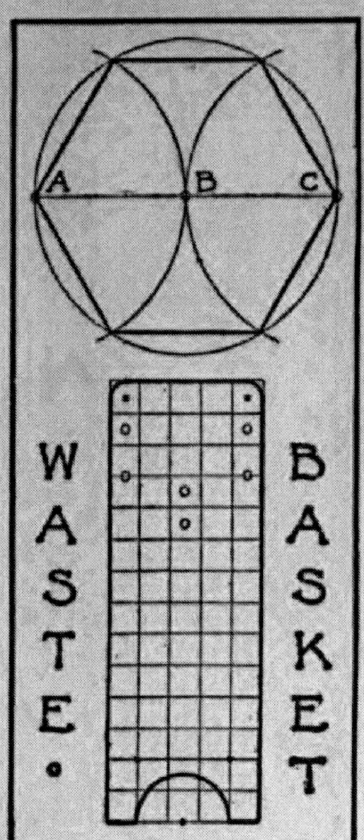

full circle through A and C. Join up the points where the circles cut each other and you will have a perfect six-sided figure, which, by the way, is called a hexagon. Remember you do not have to change the compasses once after they are properly set.

Saw out the bottom accordingly, and test the edges with the square, in order to make sure that the sides will stand straight when they are fastened on. Stain all of the pieces the color desired and finish with a thin coat of shellac, which should be well rubbed with wax when dry—all as previously described. Each side piece is now to be fastened onto the bottom board with two screws or nails, the positions of which should first be measured and marked out, so as to have them evenly spaced. When the sides are attached, lace the pieces together at the top, tying the knots inside. Go to the furniture store and get a dozen nails with large fancy heads and drive them in just to one side of the other nails, so as to cover them up and also serve as a decoration.

CHAPTER 3

Furniture You Can Make

TABORET

We are now going to make something that will require all our attention. We must remember all the mistakes we have made in our carpentry experience up to date and be careful to avoid them from now on, because this and the bench and table that follow are full-sized pieces of furniture.

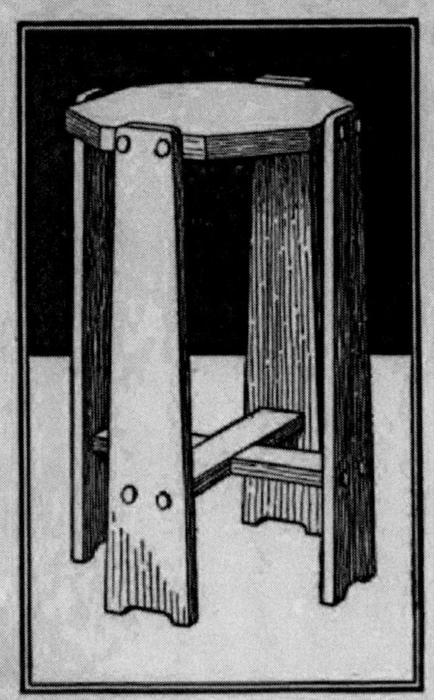

In the present case it will be necessary to find a smooth flat board twelve inches wide from which to cut the top. Get a smooth sheet of paper and draw a perfect twelve-inch square. Mark two points on each side exactly three and one-half inches from the corners, and, after joining these with straight lines, you will have a good eight-sided figure for the top. Mark this out on the wood, and carefully saw off the corners, after which plane and sandpaper the edges smooth. In order to keep this piece from warping, screw a strip about an inch thick and two inches wide on the under side, across the grain, taking care that the screws do not come through on the top side. This strip should be placed in the exact center, so that the legs will hide it when they are put on. The four legs must now be sawn to the proper taper and planed smooth on the sides. Saw out the small piece at the bottom of each one to form the feet and then round off the upper corners.

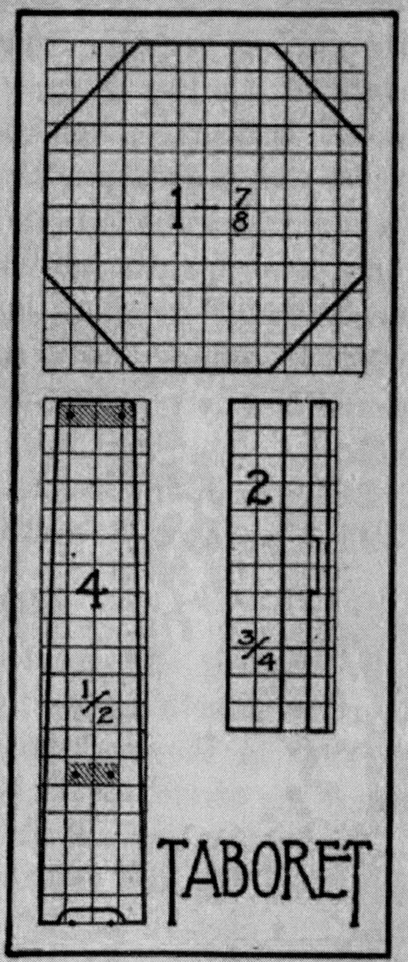

The cross-braces are now to be sawn and should be

exactly as long as the top is wide. Each of these pieces must be cut down one-half at the center, so that they will cross one another just as though they were made from one piece of wood. As soon as these are fitted nicely and tested with the square, the putting together may commence. Mark the edges of the top to show exactly where the legs should be fastened, and then nail on the legs, after which the cross-braces should be nailed in place. In order to add a little ornament and at the same time cover up the nail heads, some small round blocks should be glued on, or else nails with large brass or copper heads, such as upholsterers use, should be driven in just to one side of the ordinary nails.

Stain the desired color, shellac and rub with wax —all as previously described.

BENCH

In making this bench our object ought to be to make something good enough to use indoors—perhaps in the workshop or maybe in the attic where the wireless outfit is.

While the drawing shows the foot rail fastened in with a key and tenon, it should be understood that this may be omitted if desired, in which case the rail will be held in place by two nails driven into it through each end board.

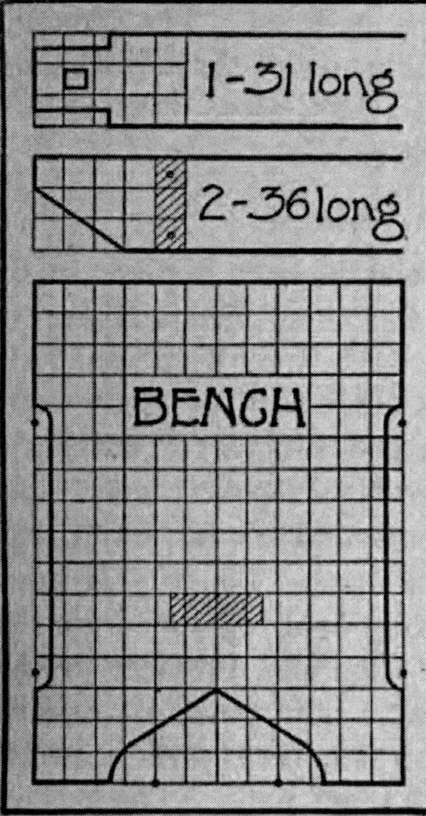

The material is all one-inch dressed lumber. The working drawing clearly shows how to mark out the end pieces. By examining this you will find that you will have to make six different curves with the compasses. This, however, is a very simple matter as the sizes and center points are all indicated on the drawing, and as soon as the curves are drawn it is only necessary to join them up with pencil and ruler, and the outline is finished. Saw out the little side curves with the fret saw and those at the bottom with the key-hole saw. Wrap a piece of sandpaper around something round and finish each curve smoothly. Next saw off the ends of the top squarely, and cut the two side pieces the same length, sawing off the lower corners as shown. Nail the top to these, carefully placing them just far enough apart so that the ends will fit in snugly between. The ends will now be fastened by nailing down through the top and in through the side pieces, after which it only remains to place the foot rail.

STUDY TABLE

Every boy and girl should have a place in the house that they may call their own. Each one should have a table where they may keep their writing materials and books and read or study when they wish to. The present design for a table is one that any careful young carpenter may make without any great difficulty. It is, in fact, a combination table and book case. The top is made from three or more boards held together by strips nailed across the under side, and, in order to hide the cracks and at the same time provide a durable working surface, the top is covered with imitation leather, fastened on with fancy nails. The legs are plain boards and are nailed to the cross-strips underneath. The shelves are simply nailed in place and the heads of the nails are afterwards covered by gluing on some small round blocks.

So you see all the difficult features in table making are eliminated.

All of the material is one-inch dressed lumber. First make the top, and be sure that the cross-pieces are not only square on the ends, but are put on so that the legs will come just right when they are fastened in place. The four legs are next to be sawn squarely to the exact length and planed smooth on the edges. Shape up the lower ends with the fret saw, and mark the places where the shelves will come. The four shelf boards are now to be sawn to the same length and exactly as long as the cross boards previously nailed underneath the top. In putting together, first nail the two legs and two shelves of each end together. Place the top upside down on the floor, and then nail on the legs.

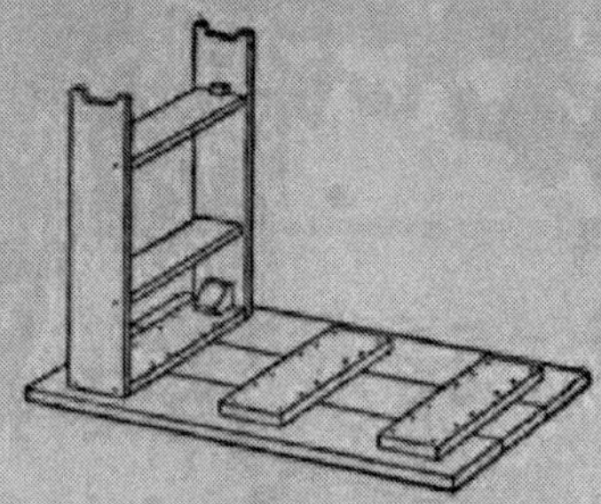

It now remains to fasten on the foot board, for which screws should be used, so as not to loosen any of the nails already driven in. Should the table now be found the least bit shaky, brace it by nailing and gluing in some small blocks under the top, and shelves on the inner side of the legs, as shown in

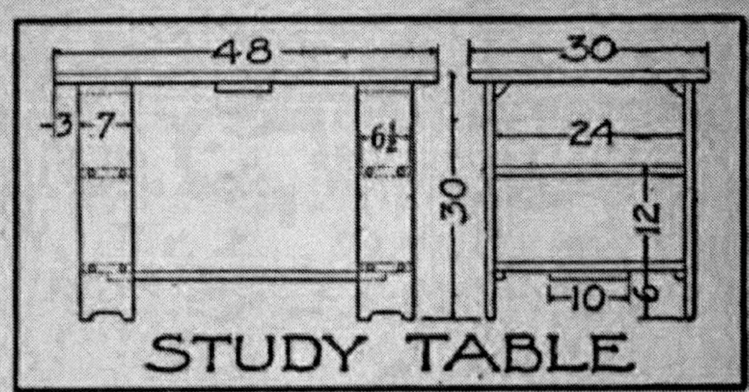

STUDY TABLE

the drawing. If it is desired to have the top look heavier, nail on strips on the under side all the way around and exactly even with the edge. After the table is stained and waxed, cover the top smoothly with some sheets of paper and then put on the imitation leather. Bring the edges clear around underneath and fasten them with ordinary tacks on the under side. Put in a tack only every foot or so until the leather is stretched evenly. When it is finally tacked all the way around, put in the fancy nails around the outer edge. Be sure to have them exactly in line and evenly spaced.

DESK WITH BOOK SHELVES

This combination desk and book rack is another piece of furniture that is especially well adapted to the needs of the student. It can readily accommodate a library of two hundred books, and at the same time affords all the advantages of a small writing desk. The construction is unusually simple.

All the lumber except the back boards is one inch thick. All connections may be made with wire finishing nails, the heads of which are carefully and deeply set, and then puttied over. (It might be well to remark that putty will not adhere to new wood unless the place to be puttied is first oiled.) The construction should start with the two ten-inch end boards, each one of which should have a little block glued on at the forward bottom corner so as to provide sufficient material to form the slightly projecting feet. Take due care to have all edges perfectly flat, and square with the sides. The amateur will often find it much easier to produce a flat edge when two boards are temporarily joined and worked up together. When these are ready, accurately mark off the position of the shelves. Next proceed with the two boards that form the sides of the desk cabinet, and work them up in a similar manner excepting that these pieces have no projecting feet. The two long top boards are next in order and should be gotten out exactly the same length and trimmed perfectly square. The upper one is a half inch wider than the one

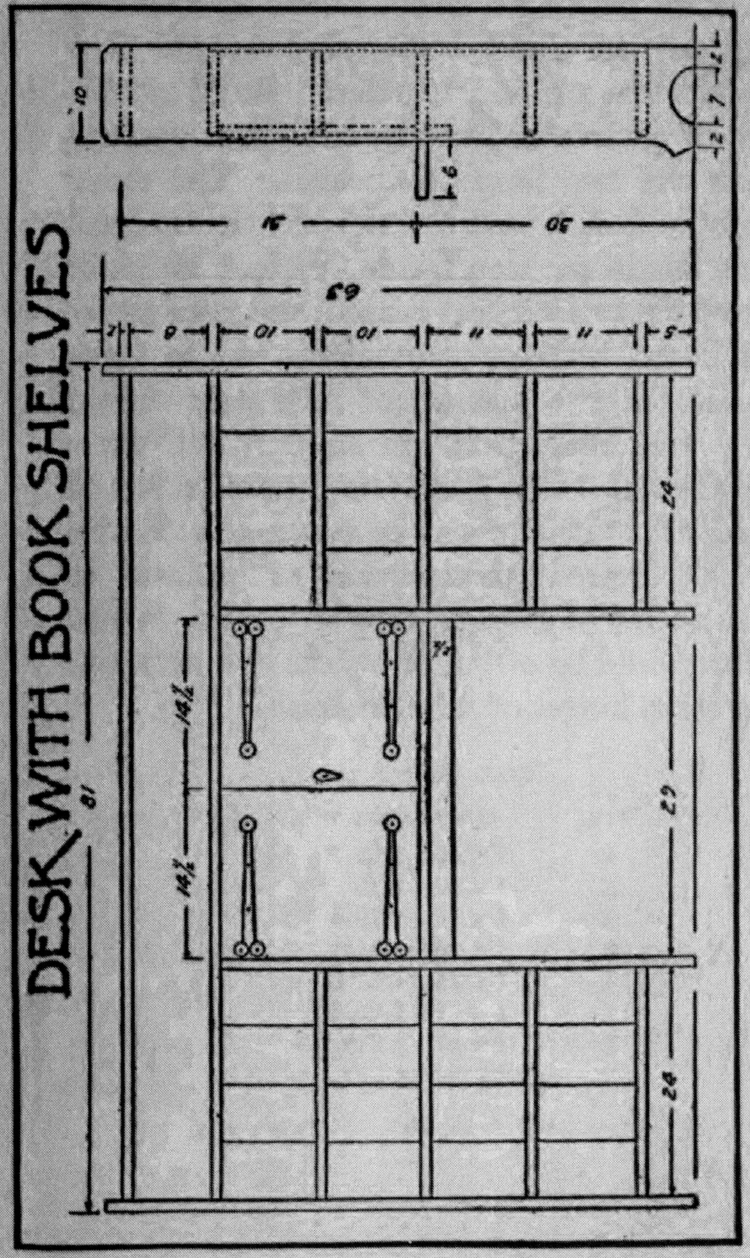
DESK WITH BOOK SHELVES
81
63
15
30
10
8
10
10
11
11
5
24
29
24
14½
14½

below it as the backing does not extend up that far. Next get out the eight shorter shelves, and then proceed with the putting together. Build up the two sets of shelves separately and then connect them with the two long top boards. The exact length of the desk board can now be determined. To secure this in position fasten one inch strips to the sides of the two vertical boards, and then screw the desk board to these with screws set in from underneath. A two and a half inch strip should then be placed underneath to support the overhanging portion. The back boards should be of about half inch stuff and may be attached with wire nails. Any desired arrangement of shelves or pigeon holes for stationery can be placed inside. Each door should be of but one piece and attached with long strap hinges of suitable finish.

MILL BILL

PCS.	DIMENSIONS
2	1 x 10¼ x 64
2	1 x 10¼ x 52
2	1 x 10 x 79½
8	1 x 9¾ x 24½
1	1 x 16 x 29½
1	1 x 2½ x 29½
2	1 x 15 x 21½
8	½ x 6¼ x 47½

PLATE-RACK

In judging a plate-rack, the imagination should always supply a few pretty plates and hang some half-dozen dainty cups on the small brass hooks on the under side of the narrow shelf. The present

design is quite small, and is intended to accommodate about a score of pieces with which you feel particularly intimate.

The back consists of but one piece, relieved around the edges with a few simple curves, which, however, on account of their simplicity, must be worked out true to line and square on their edges. This also applies to the three openings, which will first be roughed out with the scroll-saw. The shelf will then be made and supplied with a small square strip on top along the front edge, to keep the contents from slipping off. As soon as the two brackets are ready, the whole may be put together,

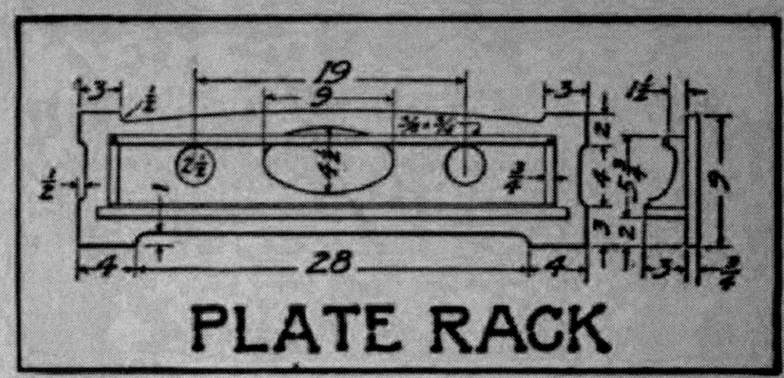

using screws set in from behind, and glue, then adding the guard-rail.

MILL BILL

PCS.	DIMENSIONS
1	¾ x 9½ x 36½
1	¾ x 3¼ x 34
2	¾ x 3 x 5½
1	⅜ x ¾ x 33
1	¼ x ¼ x 33

WALL SHELVES

The only decorative feature of the useful wall shelves shown below is the set of imitation hinges cut from polished brass, which brighten up the whole structure. If such hinges cannot be purchased, the reader will not find it a very difficult task to cut some from soft brass plate, the necessary amount of which will cost only a few cents. A cold-chisel may be used in cutting, provided a liberal margin is left for filing, otherwise a metal saw, such as jewelers use, will be necessary.

The construction is so simple that little need be said in this regard. The ends and shelves should first be made and connected, after which the back

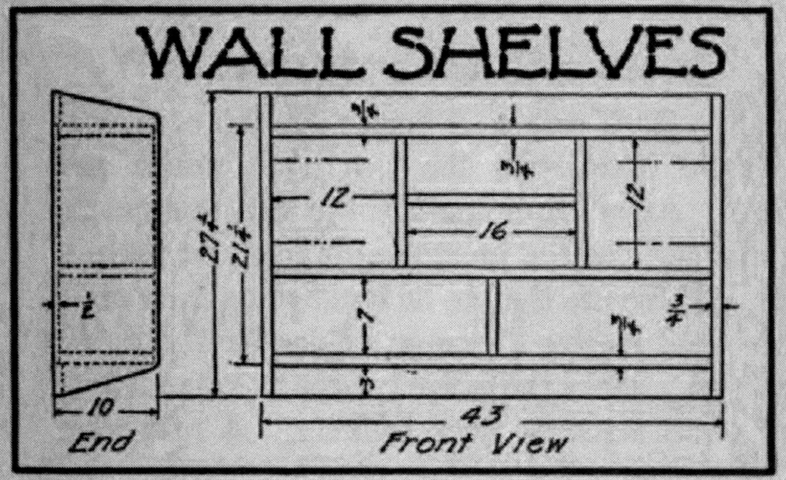

should be nailed in place. The connections of the upper two shelves may be made by means of small blocks glued and nailed in the corners of the two compartments. Use glue on all joints.

The portions of the back that extend above the top and below the bottom shelf, should be made of strips thick enough to hide completely the end wood of the main portion of the back. The doors are next made ready, and may be of single pieces, or they may be arranged to contain a small panel in the center.

Mill Bill

PCS.	DIMENSIONS
2	¾ x 10¼ x 28
3	¾ x 10 x 42
2	¾ x 3¼ x 42
2	¾ x 12¼ x 12¼
2	¾ x 10 x 12¼
1	¾ x 10 x 16½
4	½ x 11 x 22

CLOCK-CASE AND BOOK-RACK

For this clock-case and book-rack the construction should start with the two ends, which are identical. After trimming them to size, accurately mark out and cut the mortises for top and bottom boards. These are then to be tenoned on their ends to match and receive the square holes for the tightening-keys. Make the curved strips at top and bottom of pieces separate from backing. A rear edge

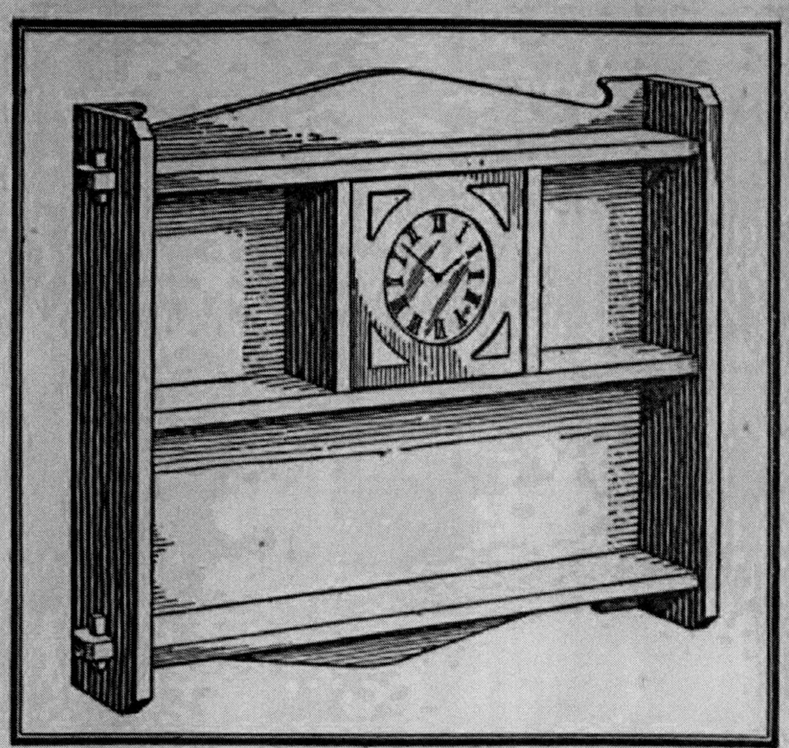

of both the top and bottom pieces will have to be notched out to fit in the backing. (See end view.) Fit the two ends and shelves together, then nail on backing, after which place the intermediate shelf. Work up curved strips at top and bottom from heavier material than backing and secure in place with nails set in from behind. The two vertical pieces that form the sides of the clock-case are now in order, after which the face should be fitted.

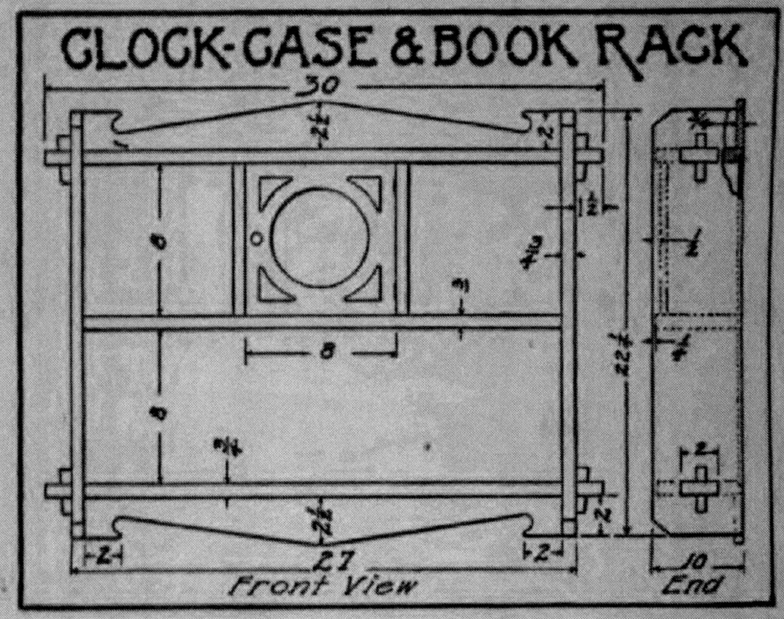

MILL BILL

PCS.	DIMENSIONS
2	¾ x 5¼ x 23
2	¾ x 5 x 30½
1	¾ x 5 x 26
2	¾ x 8½ x 8½
2	¾ x 3 x 26
2	½ x 9 x 27

CHEST

Old-fashioned, moth-proof chests, made of red cedar, have become quite popular in recent years. These may be made very attractive, and are often used in the bedroom as seats. While the dimensions for the chest here given are for a good average size, it would be well before proceeding with the construction to consult personal requirements and make any necessary alterations. The interior may be provided with a tray, as in a trunk, divided into as many compartments as desired.

The greatest difficulty in constructing a chest of

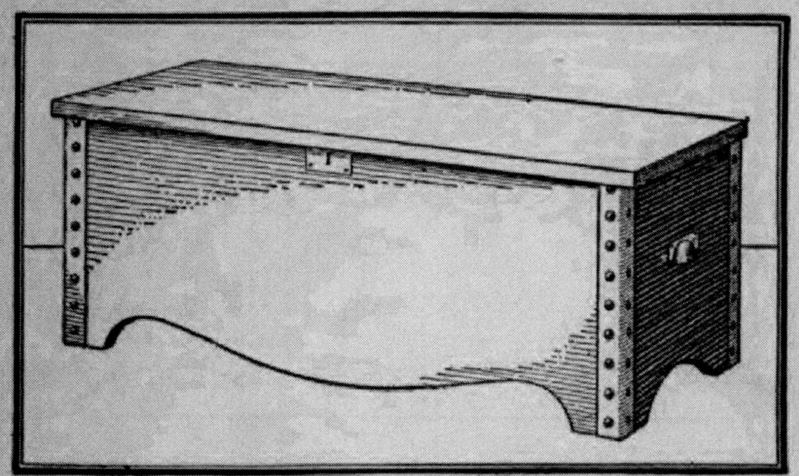

this sort is in gluing up boards for the wide top and sides. If wide pieces of lumber can be obtained, by slightly modifying the dimensions of the chest so as to make use of them, a great deal of work may be avoided. After trimming up all the pieces except the top, cut the curves on the lower edges of the front and ends. Set up with glue and finishing nails, the heads of which should be set deeply and afterward puttied. The corners may be mounted with brass, copper or even galvanized iron painted black. The necessary strips of metal should be carefully bent between boards and attached with large-headed nails of a finish which will harmonize well with whatever metal has been used for the angles.

The under side of the top should be reënforced by nailing on half-inch strips around the four sides

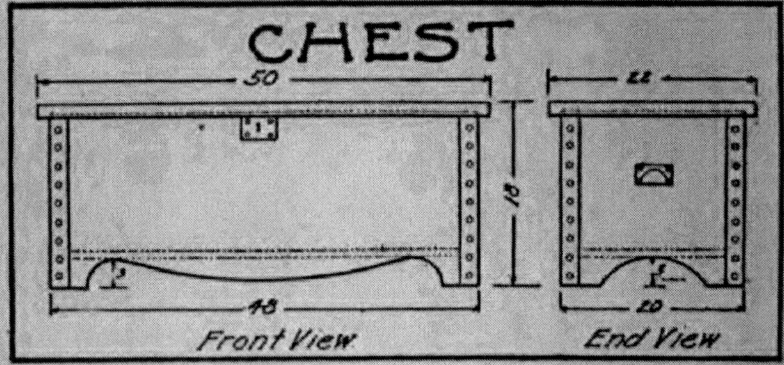

so that when the cover is down it will fit closely into the chest.

The hinges are of the butt type set inside. For ornamentation a pair of imitation ones of the same metal as the corner angles may be used on the outside. The lock and lifting handles should be of the same finish as the other trimmings. The old copper finish wears well and is good looking, and dull brass and wrought iron would also be attractive for the metal trimmings on the chest.

The mill-bill has been omitted in this case because

of the possible modification in size which may be necessary to make the chest meet personal requirements.

SUIT-CASE STAND

Something a little out of the ordinary, and altogether convenient and desirable, is the stand illustrated for holding a suit-case or trunk. How

many housekeepers have had their polished floors scratched or pretty rugs soiled from trunks!

Every guest-room should have such a stand for a steamer-trunk.

The four corner posts will first be planed up; and, after marking out the positions of the several mortises, work them down to line and finish the ends. The crosspieces will then be laid out and tenoned to match. It will be noted that the upper-end crosspieces are narrower than the side ones, in order that the top slats will just come flush with the side crosspieces. Joint the two legs of each end with the crosspieces of that end, and when dry connect the two ends with the side pieces, reinforcing the corner connections with small triangular blocks

SUITCASE STAND

on the inside angles. It now remains to place on the four top slats, and the stand is ready for finishing. It can be stained any color desired, or left in its natural color, with a coat of filler thoroughly rubbed in and then wax applied.

MILL BILL

PCS.	DIMENSIONS
4	1¾ x 1¾ x 14½
2	¾ x 4¼ x 29
2	¾ x 4¼ x 15
2	¾ x 1⅞ x 29
2	¾ x 1⅞ x 15
4	¾ x 3 x 30½

CHAIR-LADDER

It is not often that a ladder having more than three or four steps is required about the house, yet even one of this size takes up enough space to warrant us placing it in the cellar, with the result that when it is required for only a minute or two we do not think it worth the trip, and so we climb on table or chair, or whatever is nearest and most handy. The chair shown here has a good appearance and has the additional merit of transforming itself into a ladder at an moment's notice. An inspection of the drawing will make the construction clear.

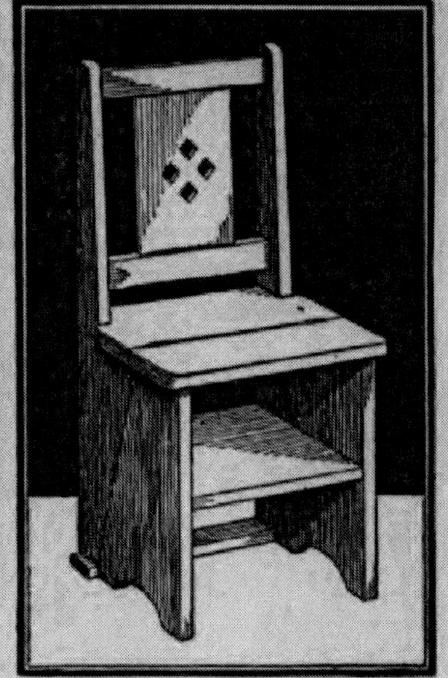

Whichever kind of lumber is used, it should measure from three-fourths to one inch in thickness. First, work out the two side-boards of each side, and see to it that when they are placed together they will form the proper shape for the side of the chair. Set the two front halves aside, and proceed to construct the entire back half of the chair. Prepare the rear portion of the seat-board and then the crosspiece that sets on the floor at the rear. The two sides may now be set up and connected, using glue and screws at all connections.

The two back crosspieces and the thin panel board are now to be prepared and fitted together,

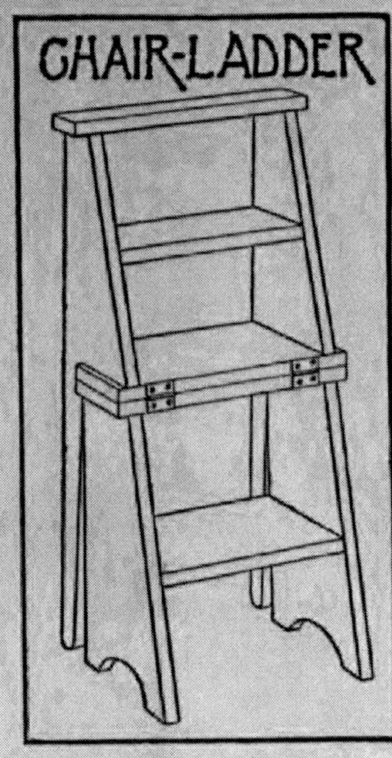

after which secure them firmly in place. The step, half-way between the seat and the floor, is now to be placed, and the back half of our chair is complete. To finish the front half it is only necessary to make the other half of the seat-board and the lower step, and with them connect the two front portions of the sides previously prepared. When the two halves are now placed together, they should form a good substantial chair, which requires nothing further than a pair of hinges to make it complete. By using blocks at the connections of the seat with the sides, and by mortising the back cross-pieces into

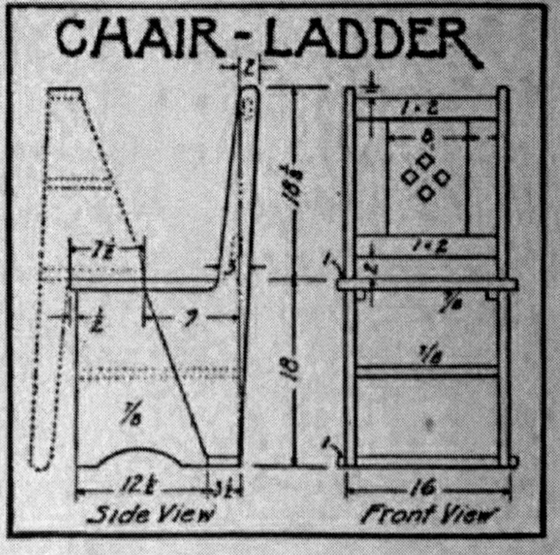

the sides, the conspicuous use of screws or nails may be avoided.

MILL BILL

PCS.	DIMENSIONS
2	7/8 x 10½ x 37
2	7/8 x 13 x 18
1	7/8 x 8 x 18½
1	7/8 x 10 x 18½
1	7/8 x 4 x 18½
1	7/8 x 8 x 15
1	7/8 x 10 x 15
2	1 x 2 x 16
1	3/8 x 8¼ x 12

TIP-SETTLE

The tip-settle serves three purposes—namely, a

seat, a box and a table. When not in use as a table, the top may be tipped up and the whole set up against the wall. The seat, which is provided with hinges, forms the lid of a very convenient receptacle for odds and ends.

The construction should commence with the two ends, which are identical in every particular. Lay out the various curves as indicated on the drawing, and remove the surplus with a keyhole-saw. The

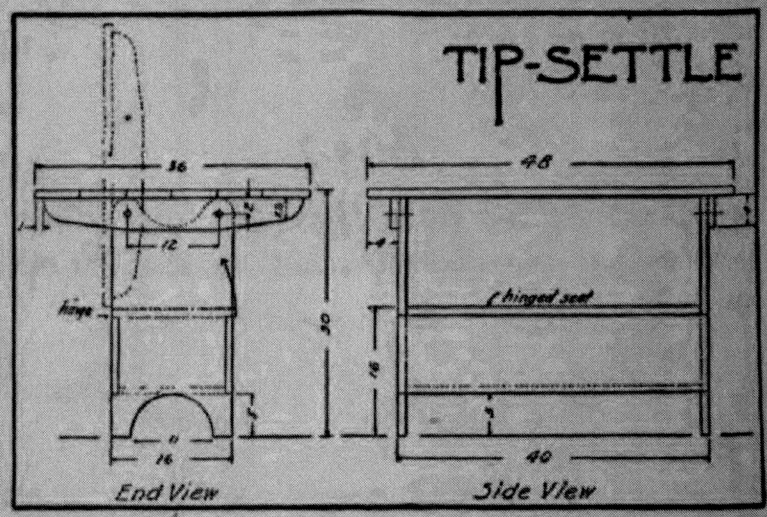

front and back edge of each end board should be notched to a depth of one inch, in order that the front and back boards may be set in flush. After boring two three-fourths-inch holes for the hinge pegs, the ends may be set aside. The front and back boards next demand our attention. These require nothing further than trimming up square and to the proper dimensions. The end boards may now be set up and connected by these two boards, using three screws at each connection. The bottom should now be filled in with one or more boards. A single board is of course preferable for the seat, which should be of sufficient width to allow it to project about one-half inch in front, as shown. After rounding the front edge of the seat, attach two cross cleats to the under side, to prevent warping. In connecting the seat to the back board use two two-inch butt-hinges. Everything thus far has been of the very simplest possible nature, but in the preparation of the top considerable care must be exercised. As this piece of furniture will be more or less subject to the weather the gluing of the several pieces of the top should be thoroughly done, in order that none of the joints will spring. After gluing the several pieces together, the top should be finished smoothly, not only on the upper side, but also on the under side, as this side is very conspicuous when the article is being used as a settle. The two pieces which are fastened to the under side of the top, and through which the hinge-pegs pass, are next in order. After shaping them up, carefully mark the positions of the three-fourths-inch holes for the pegs, taking due care that they are similarly spaced to the holes already made in the end boards. Attach these two pieces to the top by means of screws set in through the top.

MILL BILL

PCS.	DIMENSIONS
2	1 x 16¼ x 29½
1	1 x 17 x 38½
2	1 x 10¼ x 40½
1	1 x 14½ x 38½
2	1 x 4¼ x 34
6	1 x 6 x 48½

LIBRARY TABLE

The beautiful library table is of very simple design, consisting essentially of only four massive

pieces. The top and legs are particularly heavy and are of such a size that will necessitate the gluing of two or more pieces together. For one who has not had very much experience in carpentry it would probably be better to order these pieces from the lumber mill already glued. Before leaving the mill the two leg pieces should be laid, one over the other, and cut out to the proper shape by the band-saw. To facilitate this operation, the design of the legs should be laid out full size on a sheet of paper, which can be attached to the lumber before sawing. In finishing the legs, great care should be exercised to maintain all the edges sharp and square. This can be done by temporarily nailing the two pieces together and working them both up at the same time. After finishing all around, the two legs should then be separated and mortised to receive the projecting ends of the foot board. The foot board should now be carefully marked off, and as the finishing proceeds, frequent comparisons should be made with the two mortises already cut in the legs, to see how the projecting ends are going to fit. The mortises for the tightening keys should next be cut, after which the legs may be placed in position. The connections between the legs and the top are made by means of two pieces of pine, one and three-fourths by one and three-fourths inches, which are screwed both to the top and to the inside of the legs, as shown in the working drawing.

On account of its massive lines, it would ordinarily be advisable to construct this table of pine lumber, which can be stained to the desired shade. A good substitute for the heavy top may be made by providing a one-inch top and reënforcing it on

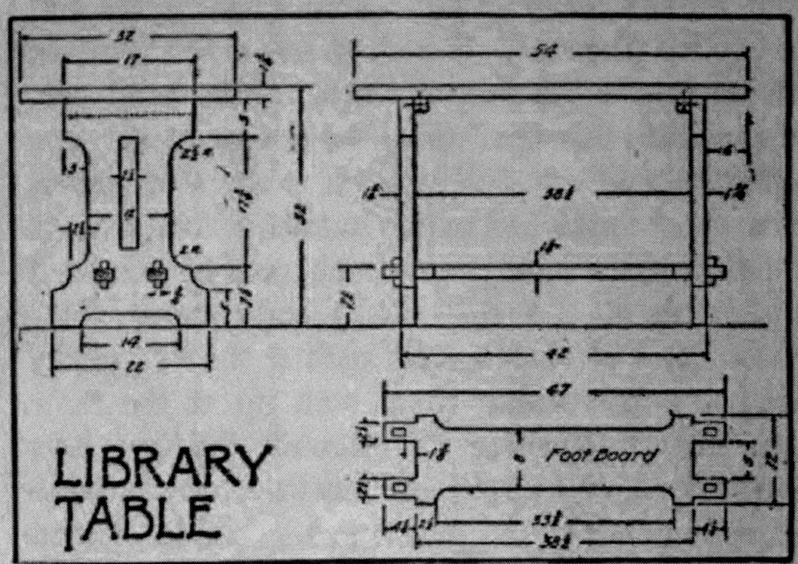

the under side with a strip of one-inch stuff and then covering with real or imitation leather. This arrangement has every appearance of a heavy top, and the large-headed brass or copper nails, which hold the leather on, give the edge an attractive appearance.

Mill Bill

NO. OF PIECES	DIMENSIONS
2	1¾ x 22¼ x 30½
1	1¼ x 12¼ x 47½
2	1¾ x 1¾ x 17½

For top, see drawing.

HALL-RACK

The hanging hall-rack fills all purposes of the old hall-tree. The mirror is quite inconspicuous, yet large enough to answer all needs of the hall. Hooks in any number or finish may be attached as

desired. If the worker owns a square of beveled plate mirror of almost the correct size, there will be no difficulty in slightly modifying the dimensions given so as to accommodate it.

The frame consists of four pieces joined at the corners by "cross-lapped" connections; that is, each piece at the place of crossing is reduced to one-half its thickness. After fitting the frame together in this manner, trim up the ends to the dull-pointed form. Mortises should now be cut for the vertical pieces at each side of the mirror and also for the thin slats with the square openings in them. These vertical pieces must now be tenoned to closely fit

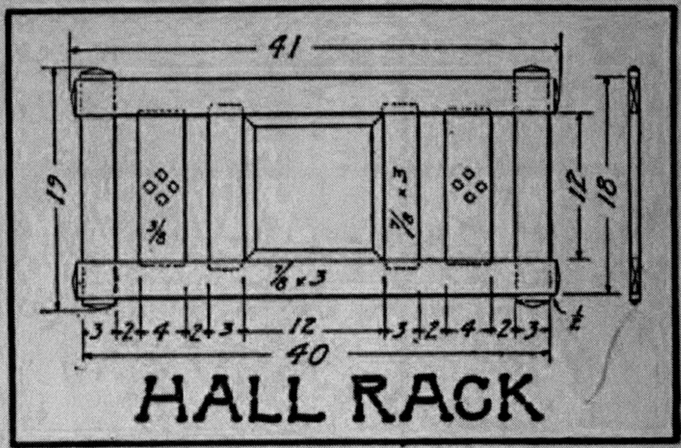

their respective mortises, after which the entire frame may be assembled. Use glue at all connections and clamp firmly until thoroughly dry. The mirror is held in place by notching out the back edges of the four pieces that surround it, so that it can be set in from the rear.

Mill Bill

PCS.	DIMENSIONS
2	⅞ x 3 x 42
2	⅞ x 3 x 20
2	⅞ x 3 x 13
2	⅜ x 4¼ x 13

COSTUMER

While the costumer cannot entirely take the place of the standing hall-rack, there are many places where it is more convenient on account of the smaller space occupied by it. In the bungalow

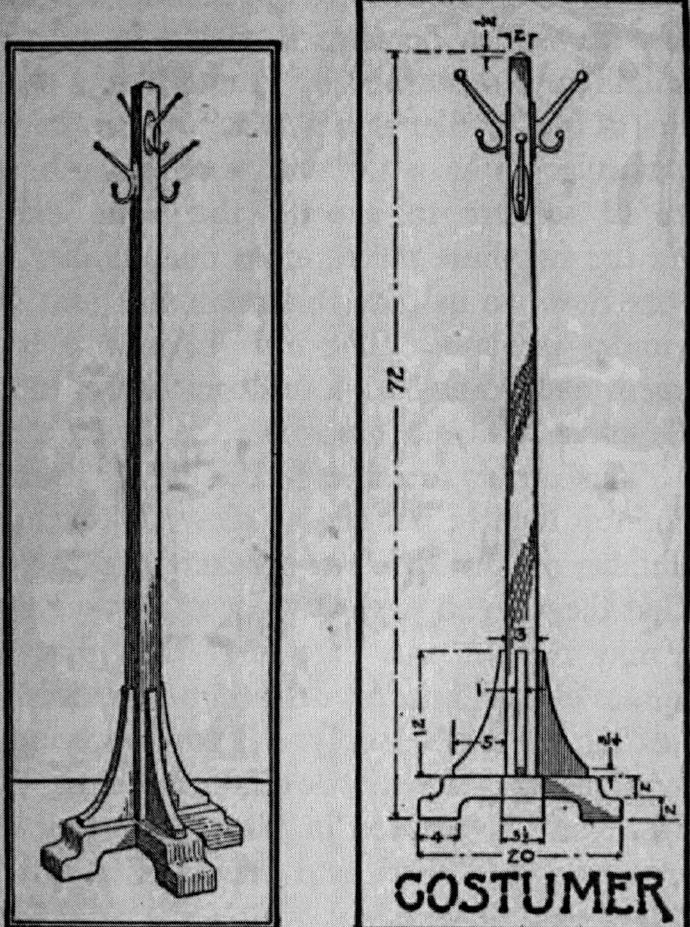

type of home, where the reception hall is so often omitted, the costumer is to be preferred. It is also a useful piece of furniture in the bed room. Our design of this article provides an attractive and easily made base of sufficient spread to give ample stability.

The two pieces which cross one another and form the base may either be sawn from two large pieces at the mill, or else formed by gluing blocks on the bottoms of two smaller pieces so as to form the feet. Be particular to have the end wood smooth, and round all corners to exactly the same extent. Where the two base pieces cross one another, cut each one down to half its thickness, and join with glue under pressure. The upright is now to be prepared, and planed to a uniform taper, except for the lower twelve inches where the brackets connect. The corners are then to be slightly rounded and the top bluntly pointed as shown. From one inch lumber cut out the four brackets, making certain that they are all perfect right angles. Everything may now be put together. Use glue, and at the toes of each bracket drive in a wire finishing nail, setting the heads deeply. Before puttying up these nail marks, place a little oil on each one. The hardware may be secured in brass, copper or dull wrought iron as desired, and arranged to suit the individual requirements.

MILL BILL

PCS.	DIMENSIONS
1	3 x 3 x 69
2	2 x 4 x 17
4	2 x 4 x 6
4	1 x 5¾ x 13

TELEPHONE-STAND AND STOOL

The telephone-stand is for use in a corner, and provides a shelf for the book.

The arrangement of the legs and crosspieces is

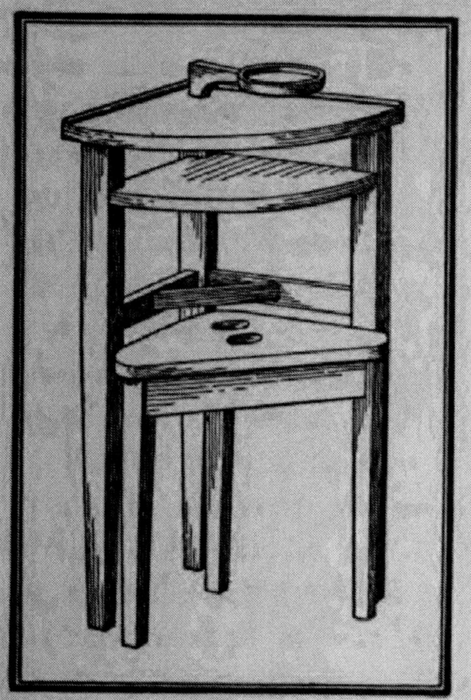

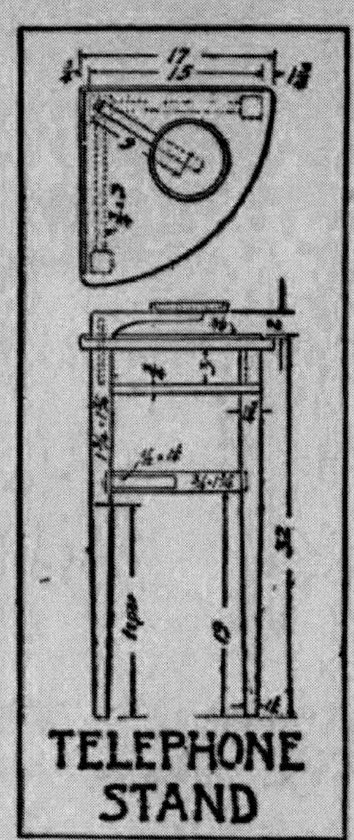

about the same as for a small square table, except that one leg is missing. First square up to length the material for the three legs, and after marking out the mortises and guide-lines for the tapering portions work them carefully down to line. The several crosspieces will now be cut to length and tenoned to match the legs. The whole should now be fitted together and the under shelf shaped up and fitted in place, after which all the connections may be made fast with glue and a wire nail or peg through each mortise and tenon.

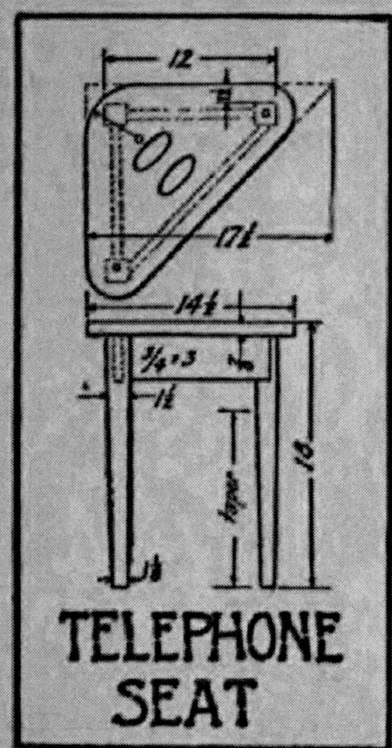

TELEPHONE SEAT

The top must have the curve true with a smooth, flat edge. To fasten, use glue and a few screws set in from below at an angle.

The small round tray may be turned out in a lathe, or may be made from a single piece, with three or four small strips of wood or metal arranged around the periphery to hold the 'phone in place. The supporting arm will be fastened across the bottom at right angles to the grain of the tray. A piece of round tubing or steel about six inches long is then securely fastened into the arm and a suitable hole bored into the stand so that the whole may swing freely.

The shape of the top of the stool for telephone-stand should first be marked out full size on paper the openings for the hand clearly indicated, after which the lines may be transferred to the wood.

The three pieces for the legs having been first squared up to length, draw the necessary lines to guide in mortising and in tapering the lower portions, all of which will then be in order. Two of the crosspieces will now be tenoned to match, and the whole fitted together so that the third crosspiece, which cannot be tenoned on account of its angular position, may be properly fitted and beveled off on the ends. Assemble with glue, and set in a nail through each mortise and tenon.

MILL BILL

TELEPHONE-STAND

PCS.	DIMENSIONS
3	1¾ x 1¾ x 31
1	⅞ x 17½ x 17½
1	¾ x 14 x 14
2	¾ x 4 x 14
2	¾ x 2 x 14
2	⅜ x ⅜ x 16

MILL BILL

TELEPHONE-STOOL

PCS.	DIMENSIONS
1	⅞ x 15 x 15
3	1½ x 1½ x 18
2	¾ x 3¼ x 11
1	¾ x 3¼ x 15

LIBRARY TABLE

The library table illustrated is an especially massive and rich-looking piece of furniture. This table has been made at a very reasonable cost, using a good quality of pine, which was afterward stained to a deep, rich brown. The top was particularly inexpensive, being made from one-and-one-fourth-

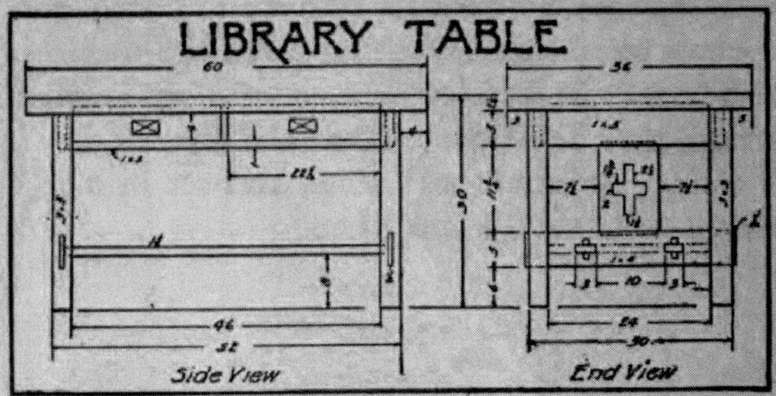

inch boards, reënforced around the edges with a narrow board, to give it a massive appearance. The top was then covered with a dark shade of imitation leather, fastened with large-head, dull-finished brass nails.

Into the legs at either end is mortised a crosspiece one by five inches, the tenons of which should project beyond the legs about one-half inch. The footboard is particularly large, and is supported by the two crosspieces by means of a pair of legs with

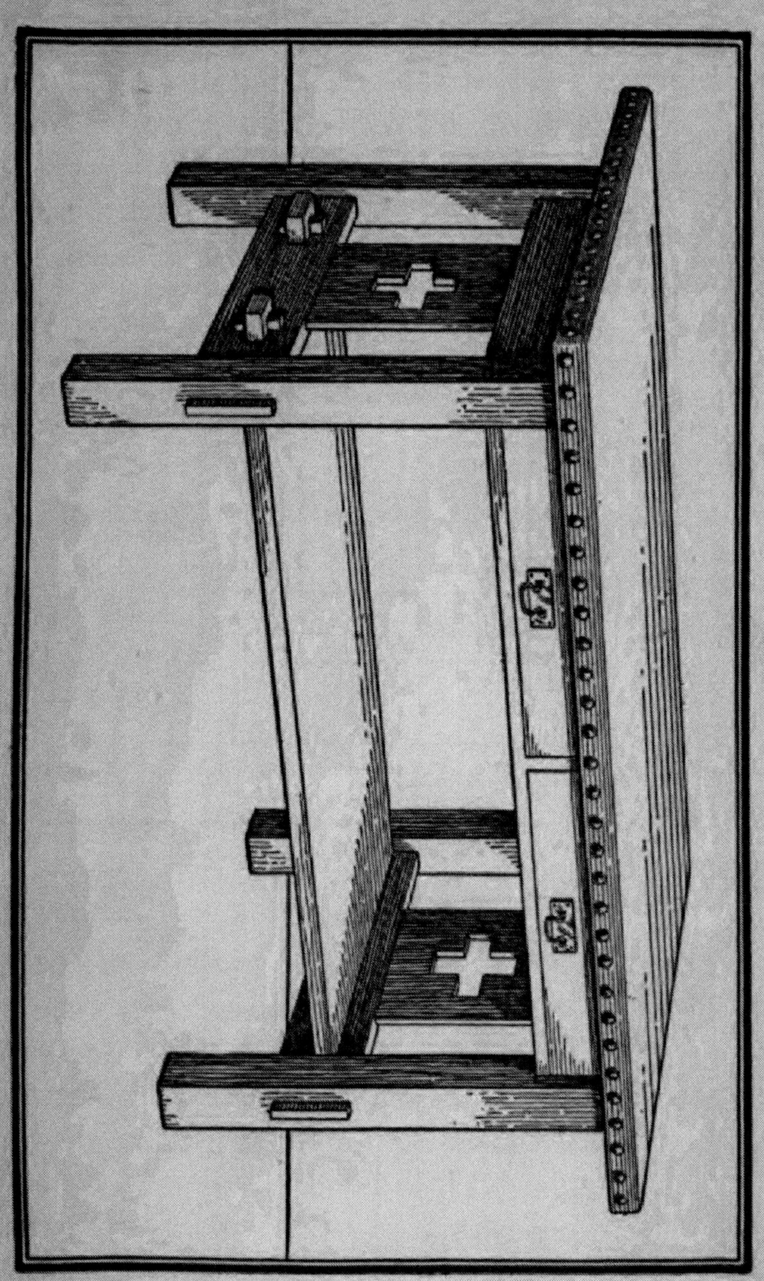

wooden keys, plainly shown in the illustration. In making this form of connection, care should be taken to see that the hole through which the key passes extends beyond the line of the crosspieces, so

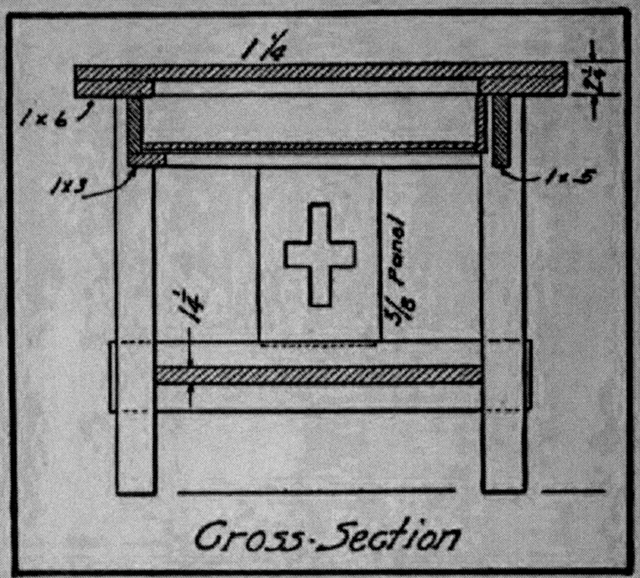

that in driving in the key it will bring the pieces tightly together.

The pieces that support the top are one by five inches, and are mortised for a short distance into the legs. To these pieces the top is secured by means of large screws at intervals of about eight inches, which pass through the upper inside edges of these pieces and into the top boards at an angle.

While there is nothing particularly difficult in making a set of drawers for a large table, it would

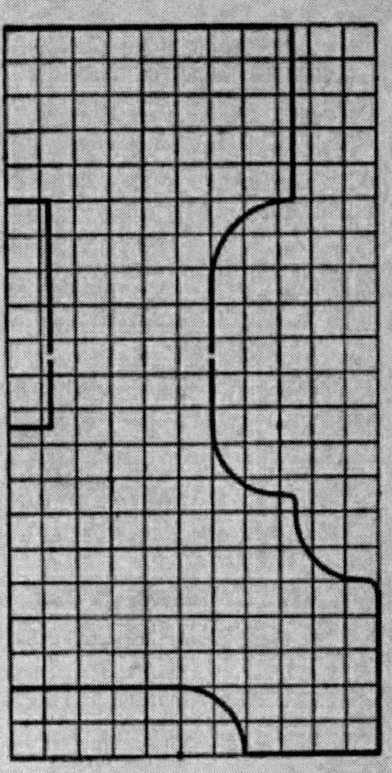

be better for the beginner who has had but little experience in handling tools to omit these, or else carefully examine some good table and note how the drawers are constructed and held in place.

The support for the drawers in front is a strip one by three inches (plainly shown in the sectional view), and in the center of the table they are supported by a piece one by five inches running crosswise.

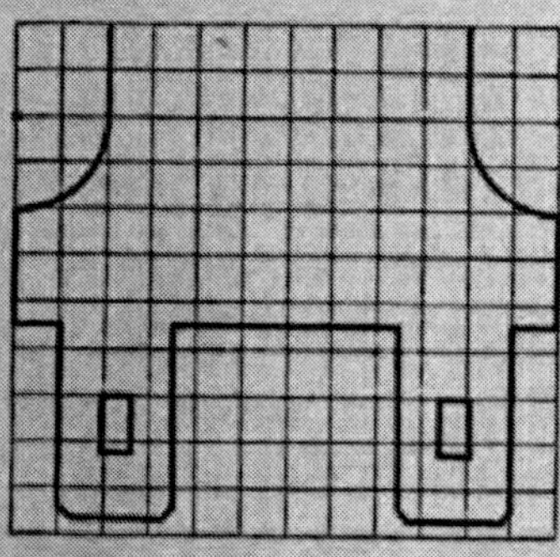

The panels are of three-eighths-inch board, in which is cut the mission cross. These panels should be mortised above and below into the crosspieces for a distance of about one-fourth of an inch. The entire table, with the exception of the top and the drawers, should be made and fitted together before gluing.

MILL BILL

NO. OF PIECES	DIMENSIONS
4	3 x 3 x 28
1	1 x 5 x 48
2	1 x 5 x 26
2	1 x 5 x 31½
1	1¼ x 24 x 56
2	⅝ x 9 x 12½
1	1 x 3 x 48
1	1 x 5 x 27½

For top and drawers, see drawing.

ARMCHAIR

We now present an armchair that harmo[illegible] with the library table just described, not only [illegible] decorative cross, but in the use of leather [illegible] seat covering.

The front legs will first receive attention, [illegible] after being trimmed up to the proper [illegible] should be accurately marked to indicate the po[illegible] of the mortises for the various crosspieces. [illegible] should then be cut and the upper ends cut down [illegible] as to pass through the arm rests and project a [illegible] beyond. The two back legs are next to be [illegible] out so as to have a tilt backwards of three [illegible] This will require a piece of lumber about three [illegible] [illegible] inches wide. When these have been [illegible] [illegible] and planed smooth, mortise them [illegible] [illegible] the front legs. The cross[illegible] [illegible] to closely fit the legs, [illegible]

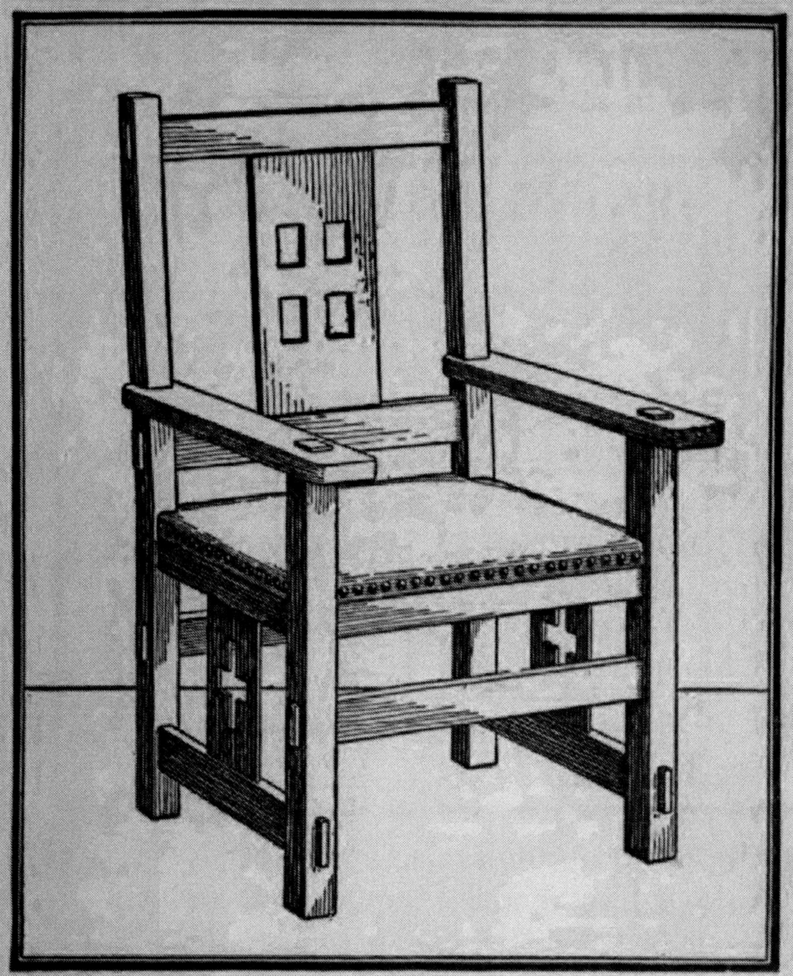

the whole temporarily fitted together in order to make sure that everything is all right.

A three-quarter inch strip is now to be fastened along the inner surface of each of the seat cross-pieces to support the false bottom. The back and side panels are now in order and should be worked out with a fret saw and accurately finished around the edges with sandpaper, after which cut grooves

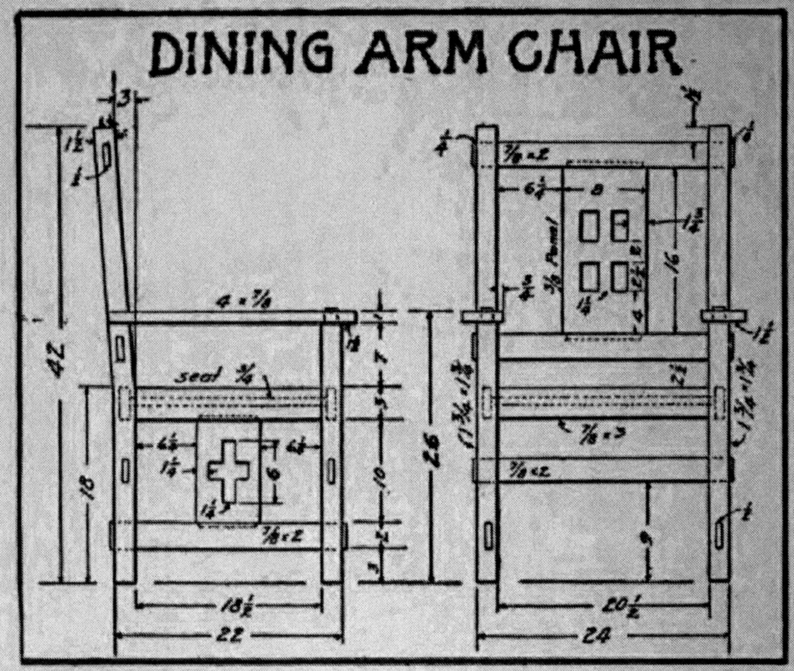

in the appropriate crosspieces so that the ends of the panels will set in about a quarter of an inch.

The chair is now ready for assembling. The best plan is to set up each side complete, using glue on all joints and clamping firmly over night. It is then a comparatively simple matter to set up and connect the two completed sides with the remaining crosspieces. When the glue has set the chair may be strengthened by boring a hole about the size of a lead pencil clear through each mortise and tenon and driving in a wooden peg coated with glue, smoothing off the ends when the glue has set.

The false bottom should be covered with a layer of upholstering material held in place by a piece of cotton tightly stretched and tacked to the outside of the four crosspieces. If the operation is successful, the final covering of real or imitation Spanish leather should be fastened on with large-headed upholstering nails evenly spaced.

MILL BILL

PCS.	DIMENSIONS
2	1¾ x 3½ x 43
2	1¾ x 1¾ x 26½
6	⅞ x 2 x 23
4	⅞ x 3 x 20
4	¾ x ¾ x 20
2	¾ x 10 x 20
2	¼ x 6¼ x 11
1	⅜ x 8¼ x 17

DINING CHAIR

In the construction of the dining chair no new feature will be encountered, and the same order of procedure should be followed. In place of the false wooden bottom a piece of heavy tent canvas may be very tightly stretched in place to take the weight, after which the seat may be completed in the same manner as for the arm chair.

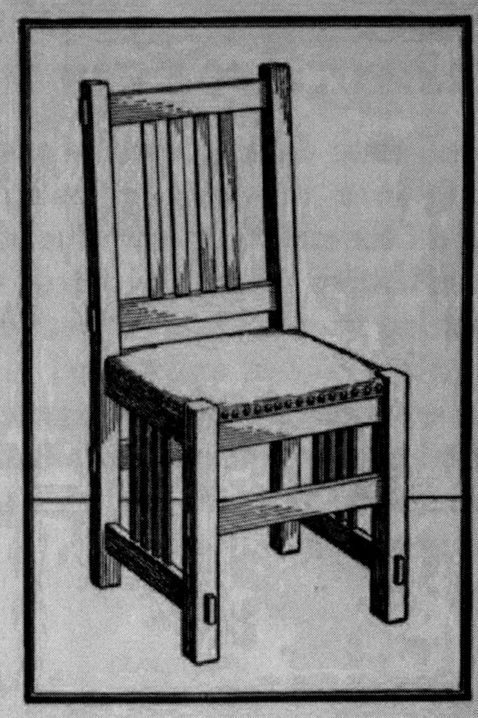

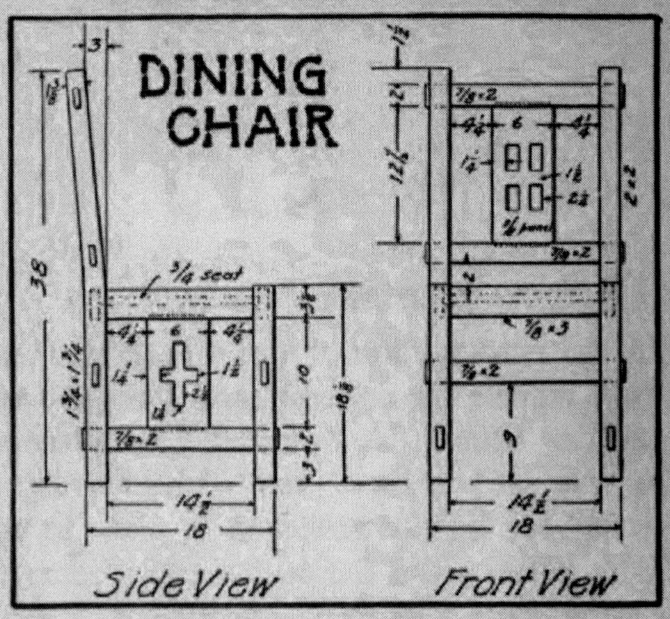

DINING
CHAIR
3/4 seat
38
18
14 1/2
Side View
Front View

MILL BILL

PCS.	DIMENSIONS
2	1¾ x 3 x 39
2	1¾ x 1¾ x 19
6	⅞ x 2 x 19
4	⅞ x 3 x 16
4	¾ x ¾ x 16
2	¾ x 8 x 16
2	¼ x 6¼ x 11
1	⅜ x 6¼ x 13½

MUSIC STAND

In the accompanying design for a music stand, with the exception of a small piece of sheet metal, bent as shown in the working drawing, to serve as a hinge in adjusting the angle of the music, the entire stand is made of wood. The main standard is composed of four strips, which form a square tube, into which fits a sliding piece having a series of holes for regulating the height of the music.

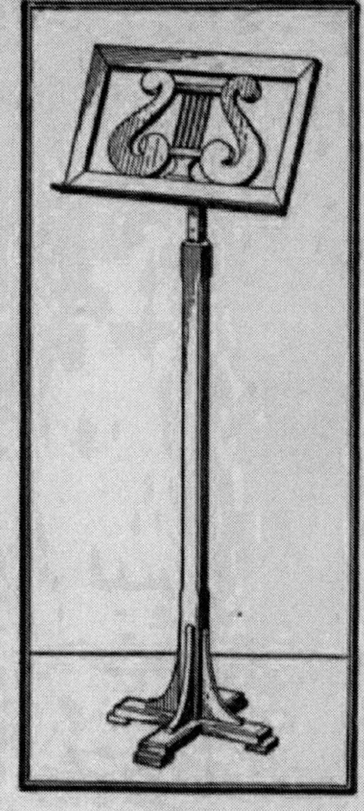

The first object in constructing will be to get out these strips and build up the main standard, which should be set up with glue and firmly

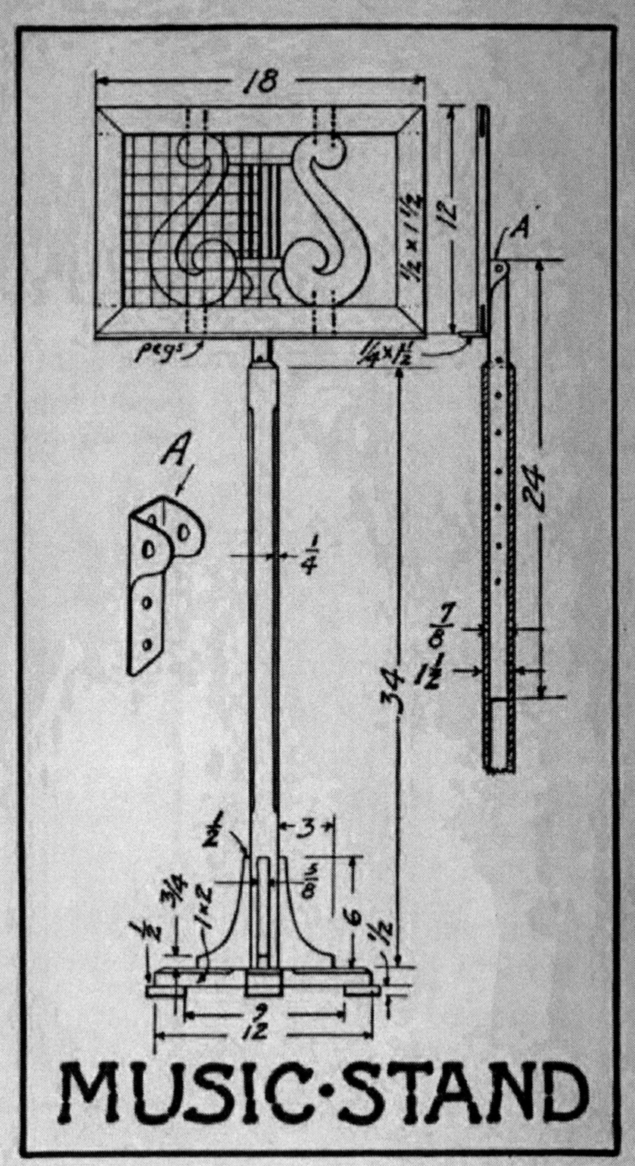
18
12
½ x 1½
A
pegs
¼ x 1½
24
A
¼
34
⅞
1½
3
½
¾
⅝
1x2
6
½
½
9
12
MUSIC·STAND

clamped until dry, after which the edges should be beveled off. The cross that forms the base is next to be built, and in order to effect the crossing of the two pieces in the center each will have to be notched out to one-half its depth. Having beveled off the ends and edges of the cross, the four small blocks may be made ready and attached, after which the four curved brackets are in order. These pieces may now be all assembled, using glue and a few fine brads set in so as to be invisible. The frame for the rack should be constructed next. The four corner connections are made in about the same way as the frame of a school slate. The small squares shown on the working drawing represent one-inch squares, and with these as a guide lay out the S-shaped figures full size on a flat sheet of paper before sawing from the wood. When these are accurately and neatly finished they should be secured in place with glue and small hardwood pegs. The small block between these figures can now be firmly placed, after which the remaining pieces will present no difficulties. (When a smaller rack is required and suitable material is at hand, it might be worked out from a single piece with the scroll saw.) It remains to add the thin strip that keeps the music from slipping down and provide the square piece that fits into the hollow standard and is attached at its upper end to the piece of metal A with a small bolt.

MILL BILL

PCS.	DIMENSIONS
2	½ x 1½ x 18½
2	½ x 1½ x 12½
2	⅜ x 5 x 10
1	1 x 1 x 25
2	⅜ x 1¾ x 35
2	⅜ x 1 x 35
2	1 x 2¼ x 12½
4	⅝ x 3½ x 6½
4	½ x 2¼ x 2¼

PIANO BENCH

The design for the piano bench provides a lifting

seat in order that the space underneath may be used as a receptacle of two compartments for sheet music. It is especially desirable if you have no music cabinet.

The bell-shaped feet add quite a little to the labor of constructing, although, as may be judged from the illustration, the resulting appearance of stability fully justifies it. This additional work, however, may be greatly reduced and a very fair result ob-

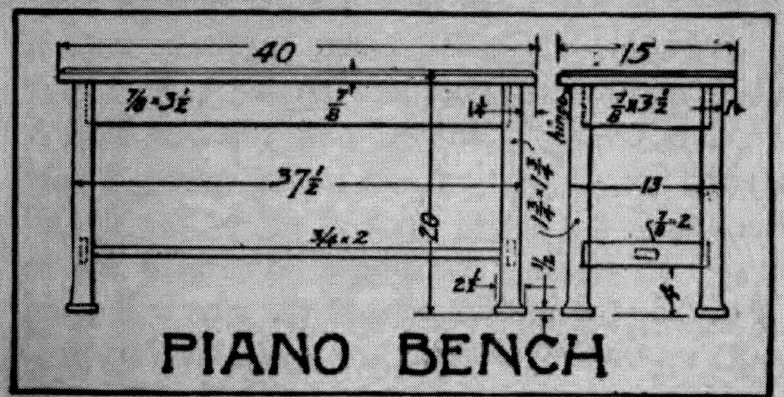

tained by first planing up each leg perfectly straight and then gluing on four small strips, from which the foot may then be formed, just as though it had been worked from a solid piece. In either case care should be taken in working around the curves, because the tendency will be to cut too deeply along where the leg begins to assume the straight form. The mortising for the crosspieces can proceed as usual after you have marked each one out accurately. The crosspieces should then be tenoned to match, and the lower one at each end should receive a blind mortise to hold the ends of the foot rail. The two legs of each end may now be connected with the short crosspieces. Set up with glue, and after testing with the steel square, clamp firmly until set. The side strips should now be made ready and fitted to the legs, after which the two complete ends may be set up and connected thereby, with the foot rail in place. A light bottom must now be fitted in and a transverse partition secured in place, all of which may be attended to with glue and a few brads. The seat now remains, and it should, if at all possible, be in one piece, nicely grained with the edges beveled off uniformly all around. In placing the hinges be careful not to set them too far in, but so that the seat will open straight up without marring the legs, and then provide a cord or brass check to prevent it going any farther.

MILL BILL

PCS.	DIMENSIONS
4	2¾ x 2¾ x 20
2	⅞ x 4 x 36½
2	⅞ x 4 x 12
2	⅞ x 2¼ x 12
1	¾ x 2¼ x 36½
1	½ x 11 x 36
1	⅞ x 15½ x 40½

MUSIC CABINET

Time was when music came only on sheets of paper, but now it comes on cylinders, on disks of

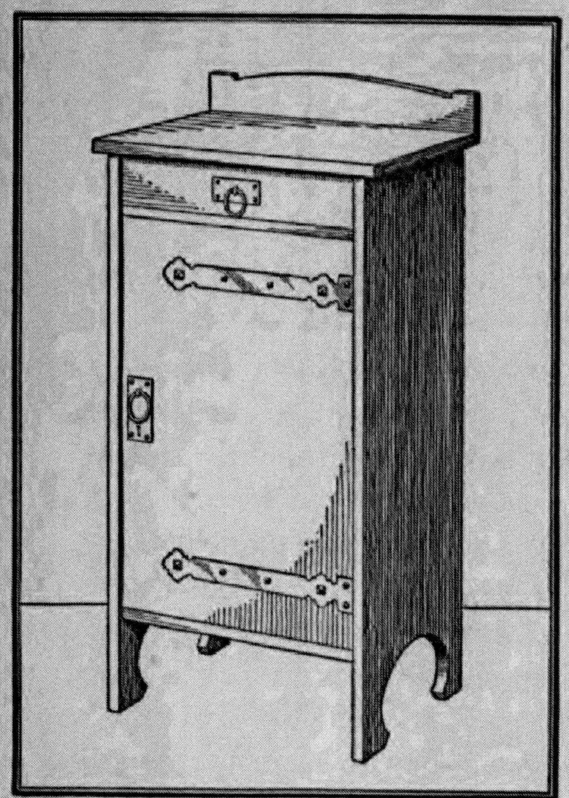

three or four standard diameters, on rolls of paper, and on thin metal, so that the fitting up of the interior of the present design for a music cabinet must be left to the individual need. If for phonograph records, due consideration should be given to the

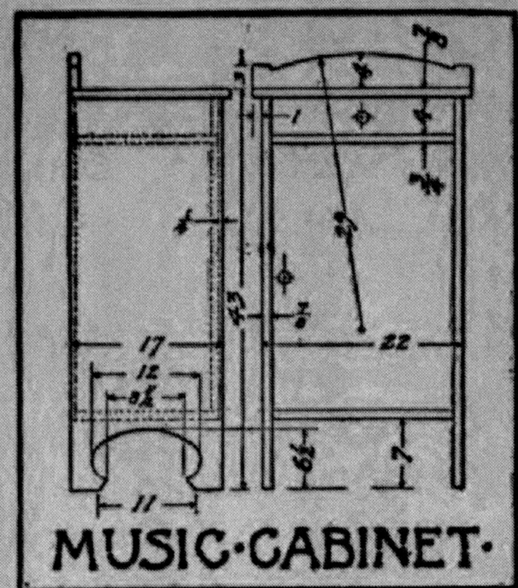

relative number of ten or twelve-inch records on hand. If for written music, do not overlook the opera scores and large volumes of standard compositions. And with the rolls for piano-players the difference due to eighty-eight or sixty-six-note rolls must not be forgotten; and the shelf spaces must be varied so as to separate the smaller boxes from the larger ones.

For the sides select two pieces as nicely grained as possible, and spare no pains to have the curves around the feet just as perfect as you can get them. This is the main decorative feature of the cabinet and the lines should be brought out clearly and with a good sharp edge. The top will require no special attention other than to have the end wood smooth and square. Likewise make ready the bottom, and then provide some thin pieces to fill in the back. Provision may be made for attaching these latter by cornering-out the rear edges

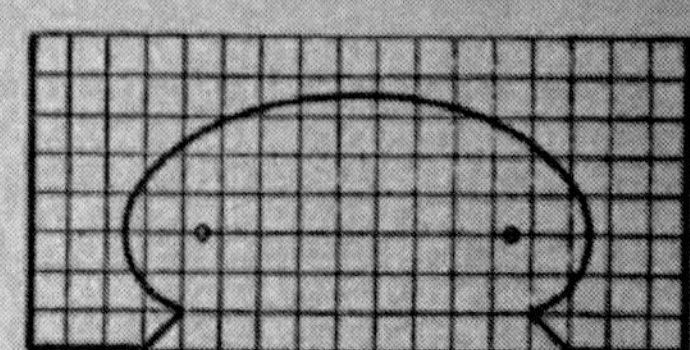

of the sides, top and bottom, for about a half-inch, so that they may be set in flush and nailed thereto. Next assemble the pieces. Provide about three wooden dowels for each connection and set up with glue, reënforcing it with a few nails set in from the inside so as to be invisible. After making sure that the structure is held square by means of a pair of light strips across the back, clamp firmly until the glue sets. (In gluing end wood always apply a preliminary coat as a filler.) The back is now in order, after which the strip across the front and guides for the drawer can be placed, and the drawer itself fitted. The details of making a drawer can hardly be given here, and in any case they can best be learned from actual inspection. The door now remains. A regular paneled one may be provided, or the plain one illustrated may be used. Such a door is relieved by trimming it with long imitation strap hinges in brass or copper, which the worker may cut from the sheet metal purchased from any arts-and-crafts supply house.

MILL BILL

PCS.	DIMENSIONS
2	7/8 x 17 3/4 x 43
1	7/8 x 18 1/4 x 24 1/2
2	3/4 x 16 1/2 x 21
1	3/4 x 4 1/4 x 25
2	1/2 x 11 x 36
1	3/4 x 20 1/2 x 30

LOG BASKET

The log basket is not only designed for carrying in the wood but also to serve as a wood box.

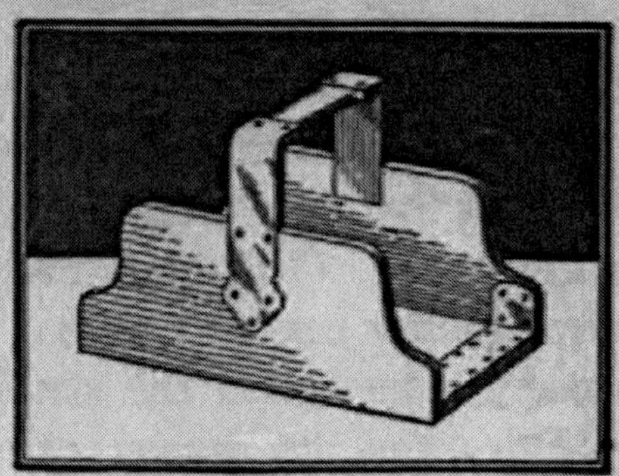

From any machinery or arts-and-crafts supply house strips of brass or copper may be obtained very reasonably. A pair of tin snips and a file will do all the shaping, and the punching or drilling of the holes will prove a very simple matter. The metal may be burnished with emery and then lacquered, but usually the oxidized appearance that comes with time and use is much more attractive.

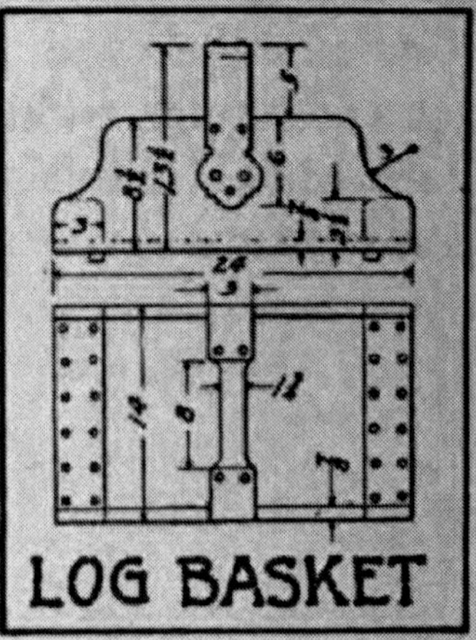

It is very desirable that the wood be of oak or other durable variety. The bottom has only to be squared up and reënforced with a pair of strips screwed across the under side. The two sides should be accurately marked out and carefully worked down to line, after which each should be mortised or notched out so as to make a good connection with the handle uprights, which are now in order. As soon as the top piece is shaped up so as to afford a comfortable grip the whole may be put together and stained. The addition of the metal trimmings will complete the basket.

MILL BILL

PCS.	DIMENSIONS
2	⅞ x 9 x 24½
1	⅞ x 13 x 24½
1	⅞ x 3¼ x 14½
2	⅞ x 3¼ x 8
2	⅞ x ⅞ x 14½

NEWSPAPER BASKET

Every housekeeper will appreciate a newspaper-basket. There seems to be no place anywhere in the house especially made for the bulky modern newspaper, and particularly the Sunday edition. And then there is that eternal question, "Where is yesterday morning's paper?"

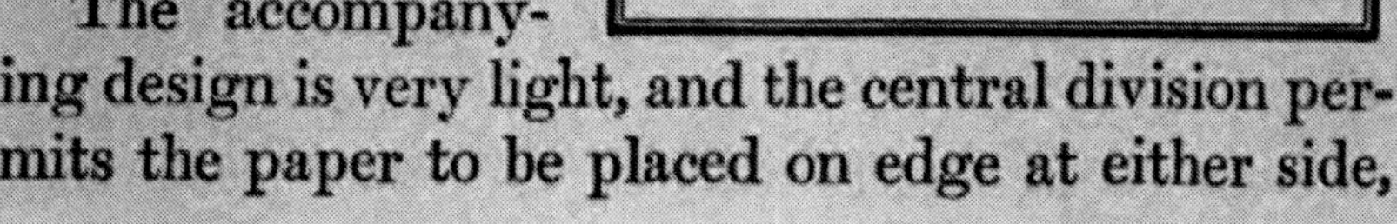

The accompanying design is very light, and the central division permits the paper to be placed on edge at either side,

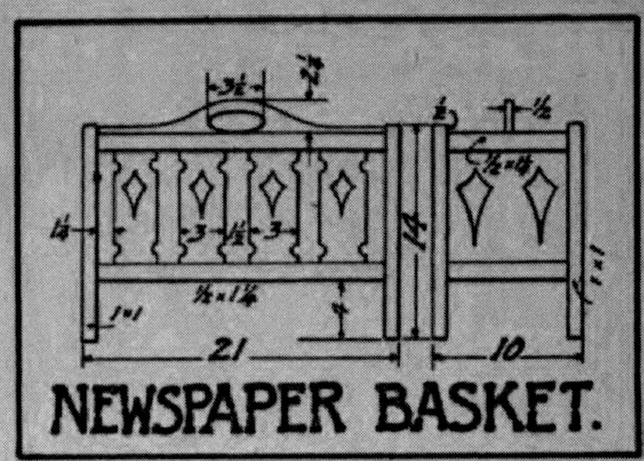

with but the one original fold. A handle is provided, so that the basket may be readily moved about.

On account of its lightness some little care will be necessary in handling the various pieces. Start with the four corner posts, and, after trimming them up, mark out and cut the several mortises. Then tenon the crosspieces to match, but instead of mortising them to hold the side slats and end boards, merely corner them out, so that these pieces may be set in flush. After making the two end boards, the two entire ends may be assembled and securely glued. Next connect them with the longer strips, and then prepare the side slats and secure them in place with glue and small brads, from the inside.

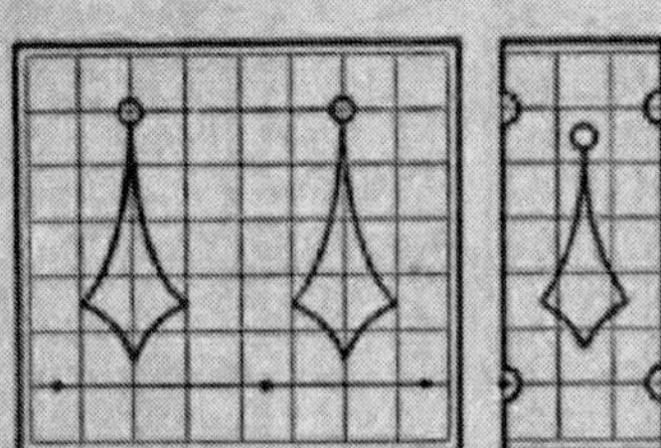

The bottom may be of very thin wood or very heavy cardboard. The central division is now to be fitted, and after shaping the handle it should be securely fastened to the bottom and ends.

MILL BILL

PCS.	DIMENSIONS
4	1 x 1 x 14½
4	½ x 1⅜ x 21
4	½ x 1⅜ x 10
1	½ x 12 x 20
1	⅜ x 9 x 20
8	¼ x 3¼ x 8
2	¼ x 8½ x 8

BOOK STAND

The purpose of the accompanying book stand is to accommodate the current books that are being read and have not yet found their way to the library. Being light and easily moved about, it is a great convenience in the living room.

First trim the material for the four legs up to length and size, then plane it to a uniform taper, after which make the mortises for the crosspieces just under the top. Tenon these to match, and fit the whole temporarily together, after which the small shelf can be prepared and fitted in place.

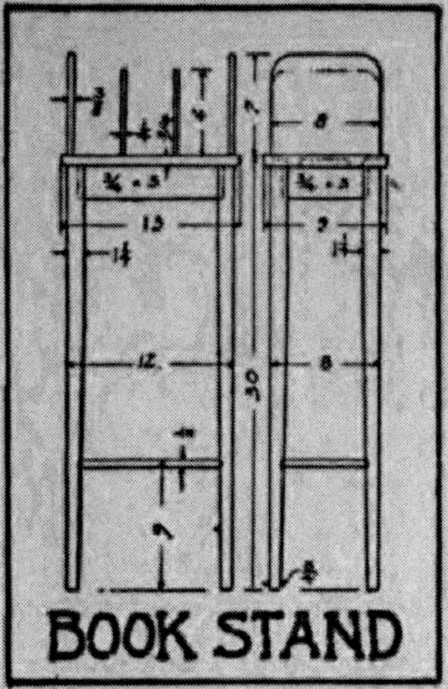

BOOK STAND

This piece is fastened to the legs by cutting off its corners slightly and then notching out the inner corners of the legs to match, all of which must be accurately done, or the legs will not stand parallel. You can now set up the whole with glue, and put in a few small brads where they will not be seen. Clamp firmly while setting.

The top is now in order, and after squaring it up to size mark off the four vertical pieces. Cross grooves must now be cut so that these latter will sit in; and, in order to give added strength, at two points for about an inch each groove should be mortised clear through.

Two corresponding tongues will then be formed on each of the four vertical pieces, and when the whole is set up with glue no danger need be feared from hard usage. It now remains only to place the top and secure it with glue and a few screws set in at an angle from below.

MILL BILL

PCS.	DIMENSIONS
4	1¼ x 1¼ x 30
1	¾ x 9¼ x 13½
1	½ x 7½ x 11½
2	¾ x 3¼ x 11
2	¾ x 3¼ x 8
2	⅜ x 8¼ x 8½
2	¼ x 8¼ x 7½

MAGAZINE STAND

The construction of the magazine stand could not be simpler; merely two side boards with shelves between, yet by cutting the sides to a suitable taper and making a few simple openings a pleasing design is obtained. The end of each shelf is supported by four dowel pins, the heads of which project slightly and are rounded off.

The first point is to mark out accurately and lightly on the two side pieces not only the outline but all openings, the positions of the shelves and the dowel pins. After removing the surplus material, a hole should be bored at the end of each slot and in each corner of the rectangular opening, so that the saw point may be inserted.

In order to produce good clear outlines to all these openings, it is almost needless to state that considerable care will be necessary. The sawing

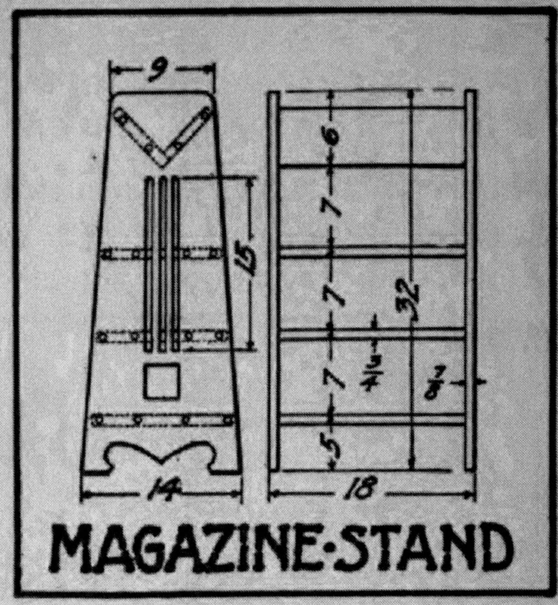

MAGAZINE·STAND

should be done from the outside so that if a splinter should accidentally be removed it will be from the inside surface.

Another small detail upon which much will depend is the need of having the dowel-pin holes bored at right angles with the sides. The shelves are all of a length. In order to get exact alignment in placing the dowels either bore clear through the sides into the shelves after temporarily fastening

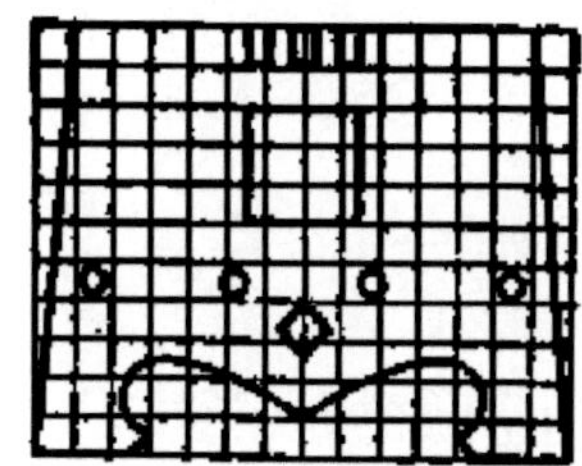

them together, or else mark off the adjoining holes on the shelf end as soon as the first dowel of that particular connection is placed.

When the fitting is all satisfactorily accomplished, give the end wood of the shelves a preliminary coat of glue as a filler, and when this has dried, set up permanently, clamping all connections firmly overnight.

MILL BILL

PCS.	DIMENSIONS
2	⅞ x 14½ x 33
1	¾ x 11 x 17
1	¾ x 12 x 17
1	¾ x 13½ x 17
1	¾ x 7 x 17

SEWING-STAND

This little sewing-stand is very light and has two rings, so that it may readily be brought up close to the chair by the window. Near the top is a removable tray for the spools and needles, and on the under side of the lid a piece of leather is fastened for holding the scissors.

In making anything hexagonal, accurately set the gauge at sixty degrees, so that all angles may be repeatedly tested as the work proceeds. The six similar side pieces must first be trimmed up squarely

and to the exact size, and should have their feet formed before beveling off the edges. Next lay out the hexagonal bottom as accurately as possible with a pair of pencil dividers, and if

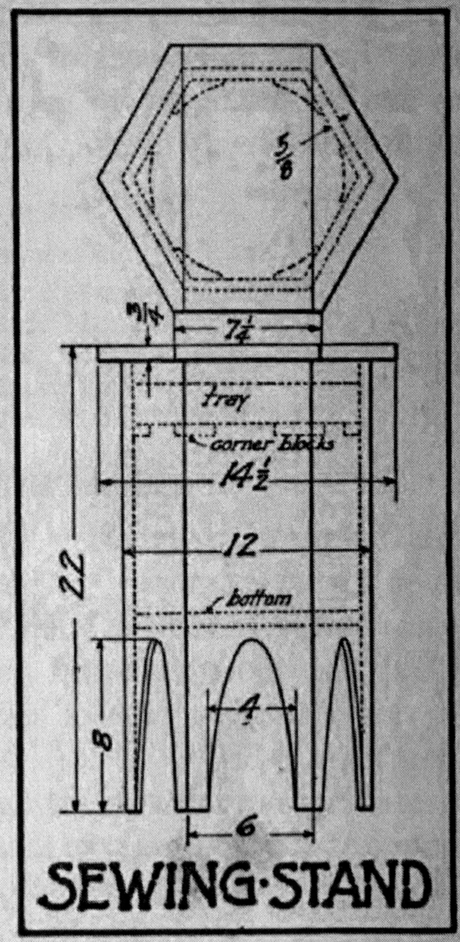

any difficulty is contemplated in assembling make a second hexagon to act as a temporary top. This latter will keep the side pieces in their proper relation while they are being fastened to the bottom and glued along the edges. Before assembling, fit everything together, and provide means for clamping while the glue sets. To strengthen the side seams and to act as a support for the tray, make six little blocks as shown in the working drawing, and fasten them in place with glue and screws. The tray may be made as deep and in as many compartments as desired. The top is more apt to retain its shape if made of three pieces, fastened with glued tongue-and-groove connections.

On the inner side of the cover a little piece of leather is tacked to form a case for the scissors, which are then most conveniently at hand when the top is raised. The top is attached to the stand by means of little brass hinges, and neat brass rings set in at the sides of the stand serve as handles, so that it can be moved about easily.

MILL BILL

PCS.	DIMENSIONS
6	¾ x 6¼ x 22
1	¾ x 13 x 7
2	¾ x 5 x 13
1	⅞ x 10 x 11½
1	⅜ x 10 x 11½
1	¼ x 2 x 60
1	¾ x 1 x 18

DICTIONARY STAND

The dictionary-stand is of simple construction, and not only holds the dictionary at a suitable angle,

finally mortised for the top crosspieces. The positions of the diagonal crosspieces will then be located and the inner corner of each leg flattened off at these points, so that the mortises for the diagonals may be run in properly.

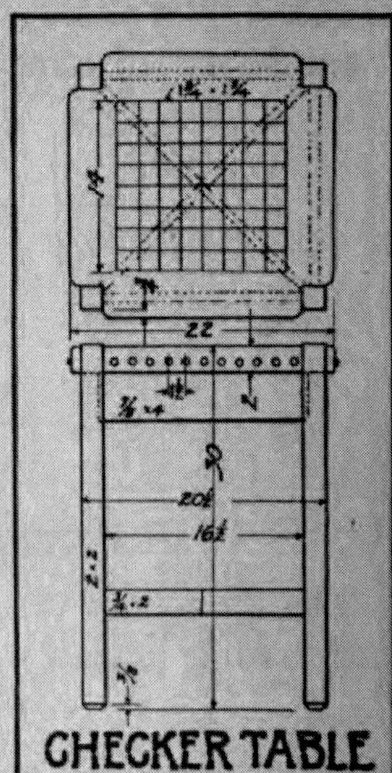

CHECKER TABLE

The four identical upper crosspieces are now in order, and will be tenoned to match the legs, after which the eight pieces thus far made will be fitted together so that the exact length of the diagonals may be determined. These latter will then be made ready, and each must be notched out, where they cross in the center, to one half its depth.

The structure may now

be set up with glue and the upper connections reën-forced with a few nails or pegs set in from the inside. While the glue is setting, the top may be made ready. This should be of two thicknesses of one-inch stuff crossed, or may be made of one thickness built up on the under side around the edges. Round all corners, and attach with screws set in from below at an angle. Use two layers of blotting-paper as an underlay, and then fit on the top covering, the edges of which should be tacked underneath with small tacks, after which the large ornamental nails may be put in.

MILL BILL

PCS.	DIMENSIONS
4	2 x 2 x 30½
4	⅞ x 4¼ x 18
2	¾ x 2 x 26
4	1 x 11¼ x 22½

TABLE

The accompanying design presents a table of considerable utility. At either end a shelf is provided for current books, and a space in the center is set aside for magazines.

In constructing the same first prepare the two side boards and, after shaping out the feet, mark out and cut the mortises for the projecting tenons of the foot board, which may then be accurately formed to correspond.

The shelf board and top must be squarely trimmed to size. Now begin the putting together. Place the footboard, nail the shelf in place, and attach the top with screws set in at a suitable angle from below. Next make ready the two overhanging shelves and the four slender brackets. Attach the latter with glue and a few brads. Place the side shelves in position, thus hiding the nails previously set to hold the large shelf, and nail them to the brackets. These nails will in turn be hidden by the small pieces to be added above.

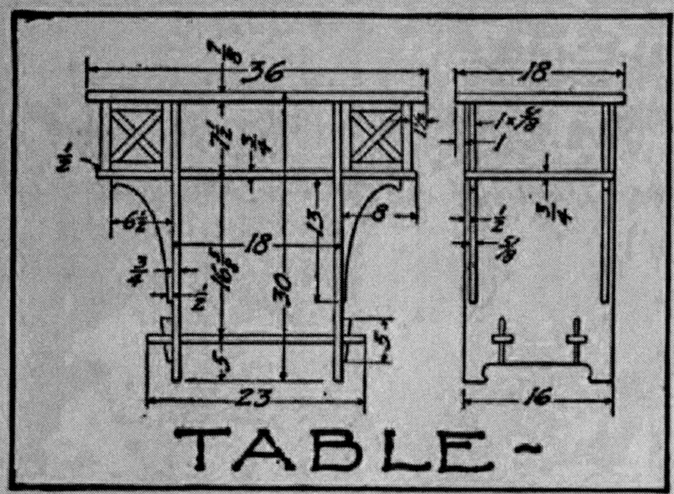

Make the outer frames of the four rectangular panels first, and see that they fit in place before going further. Place one diagonal and then put in the halves of the remaining one.

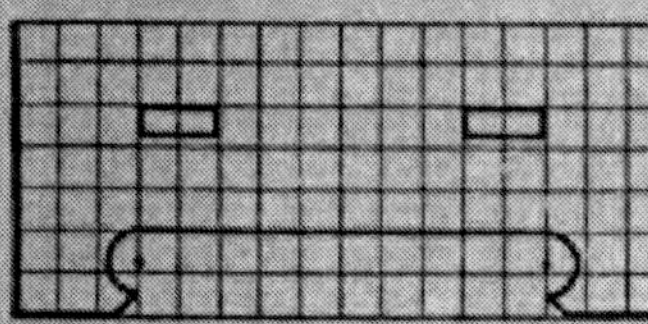

The completed panels may be secured by the application of glue.

MILL BILL

PCS.	DIMENSIONS
1	⅞ x 18½ x 37
2	¾ x 16½ x 30
1	¾ x 16½ x 17
1	¼ x 16½ x 24
2	¾ x 8½ x 17
4	⅝ x 7 x 13½
20 ft.	⅝ x 1

DINING TABLE

In constructing the round dining table the joining of the top will prove to be the most difficult part.

If the amateur has had no experience in this line, it is best to have the lumber-mill do it for him. Secure good clear lumber of fair width and, after truing up the edges, lay the several pieces on the bench and draw a circle about an inch larger than the finished top. Rough out the boards with the saw, and join them with fresh glue, clamping

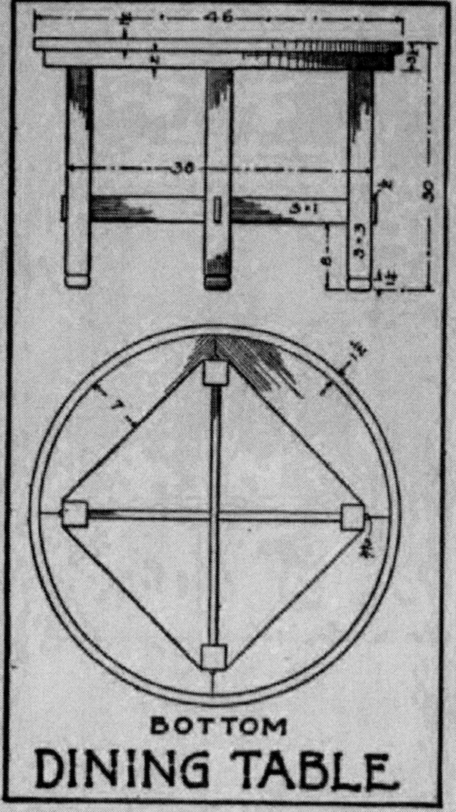

DINING TABLE

tightly until dry. Draw the final circle, and remove the surplus material with the key-hole saw, finishing with the plane.

The four two-inch under pieces are now to be prepared in the form shown on the bottom view of our drawing. Fit these together accurately, and see that the spaces for the tops of legs are perfectly square and at right angles with the top. Next attend to the legs. In forming the feet make a saw cut on the four sides to a depth of three eighths of an inch, and then finish with the chisel. Mark out the position of the mortises for the tie pieces, and cut them from both sides. Carefully determine the length of these tie pieces and tenon them to match the legs. When the tie bars pass one another at the center, cut down each one to half its width. Put the legs and tie pieces all together, and set them on the top, which should be placed on the floor, bottom side up. (Be sure that nothing is on the floor to mar it.) Fasten each leg to the top with glue and three long screws set in at an angle. With very fine sand-paper go over the table and slightly remove the corners. When sand-papering the top and legs do not hold the paper in hand, but place it on a block.

MILL BILL

PCS.	DIMENSIONS
4	3 x 3 x 29
4	2 x 7 x 32
2	1 x 3¼ x 39½
	Top, special.

BEDSIDE STAND

The construction of the bedside stand begins with the legs. Square off the tops, shape the feet and then mark off the various mortises; those for the cross-boards, which form the ends of the drawer spaces, should be let in about a half inch, and those for the lower crosspieces cut clear through. The two cross-boards and two cross pieces, tenoned to

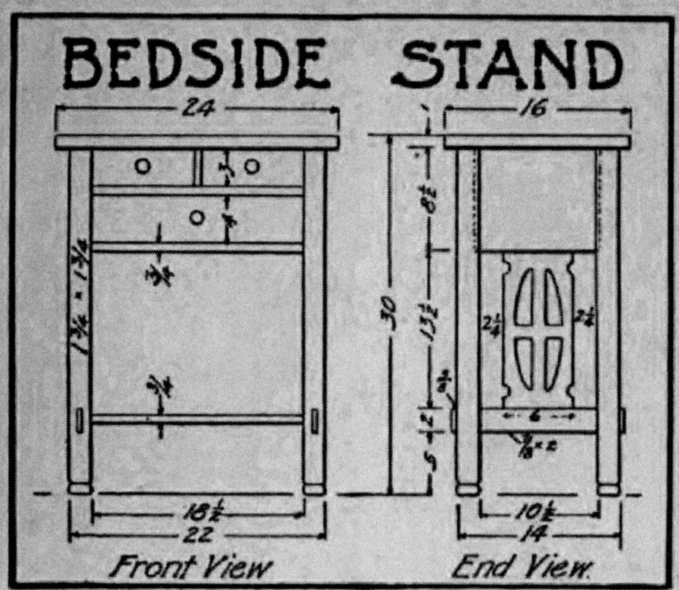

match the legs, the proper grooves cut in them to receive the ends of the end panels, are next prepared. These panels, preferably of hard wood, must be carefully cut with a scroll-saw. The two complete ends can now be assembled, using fresh glue and leaving clamped firmly overnight. The two horizontal boards for the drawer spaces and the foot-shelf are now to be gotten out with their ends squarely trimmed. As the two upper boards are wider than the lower one, their corners will have to be notched out so as to pass around the legs. The

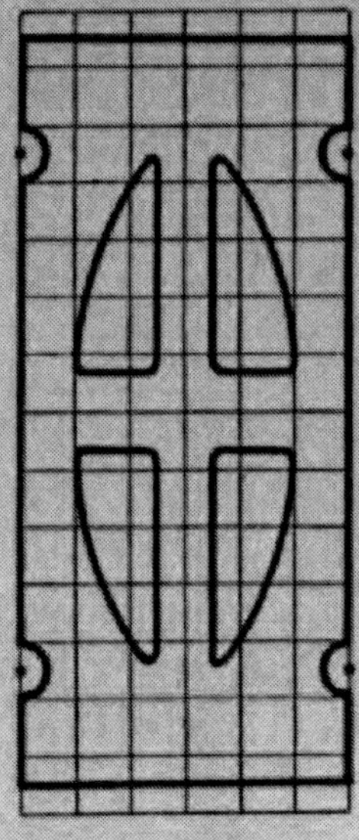

assembled sides may now be set up and connected by these three boards, using glue and finishing-nails, or screws set in at an angle from the inside. The top, smoothly and accurately finished, may then be attached with glue and screws set in invisibly. Fit a half-inch board at the back to fill in the drawer space and stiffen the table laterally. It will not be found difficult to make and fit the three drawers which complete the table.

MILL BILL

PCS.	DIMENSIONS
4	2 x 2 x 30
2	1 x 9 x 11
2	1 x 2 x 15½
2	¾ x 14 x 20
1	¾ x 11 x 20
1	1 x 16½ x 25
1	¾ x 3½ x 14
1	½ x 9 x 19
2	¼ x 6½ x 15

Also drawers.

BEDROOM CHAIRS

The accompanying working drawing presents a bedroom chair of similar construction to the dining chair with the leather seat, previously described.

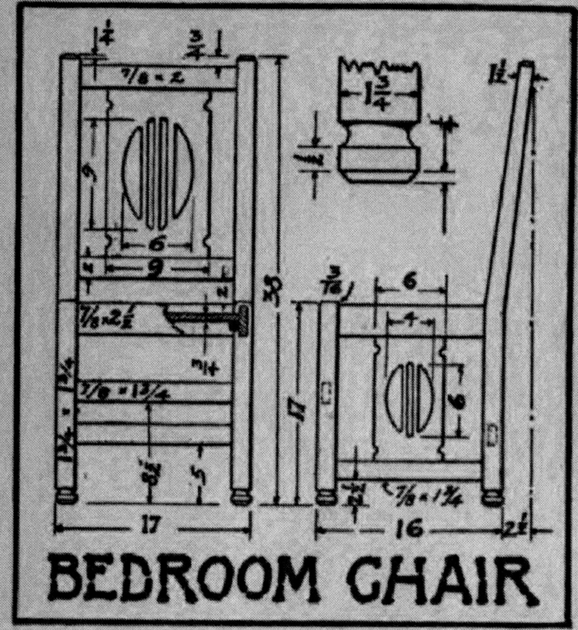

The back panel, however, is made to match the foregoing bedside stand.

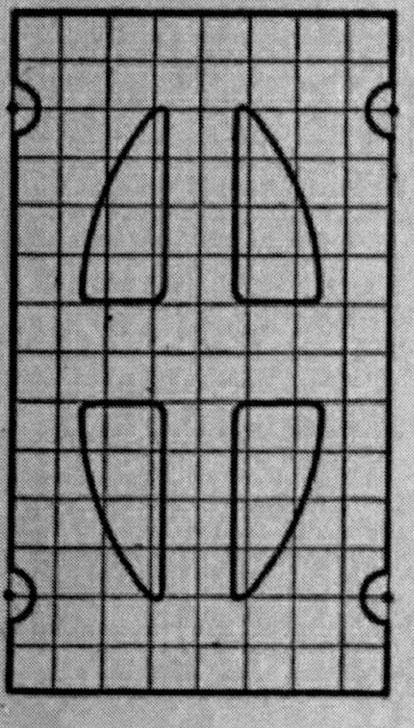

In the second chair still another form of panel is used, and instead of a permanent seat covering, a loose, flat cushion is provided, the covering of which should be the same as or harmonize with the bedroom hangings.

The construction should commence with the two rear legs, which, on account of their bend, will have to be sawed from two pieces about three inches in width. When planed smoothly down to line, mark out the guide-lines for the top, feet, and mortises, after which shape up the upper ends and feet. The front legs will now be made ready and similarly mortised, noting, of course, that the front crosspiece is placed higher than the rear one.

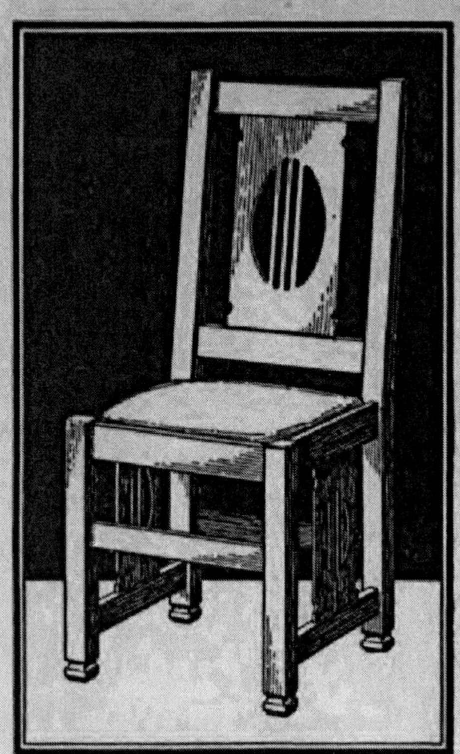

The two crosspieces of each side are next in order, and should be tenoned to fit the mortises just made, after which a groove will be cut in each to receive the ends of the side-panel boards. These will then be sawed out, taking due care to bring out the lines sharp and clear. The two complete sides may now be set up with glue and securely clamped. The four rear and two front crosspieces are now to be accurately marked out and tenoned to match the sides, after which the thin back-rest will be prepared as carefully as were the side panels. It now only

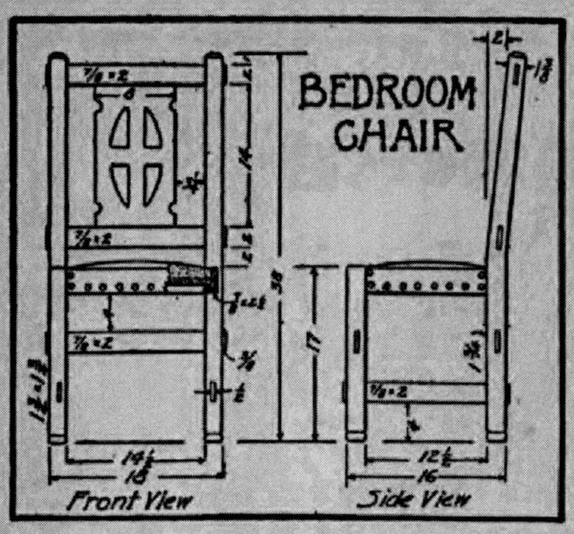

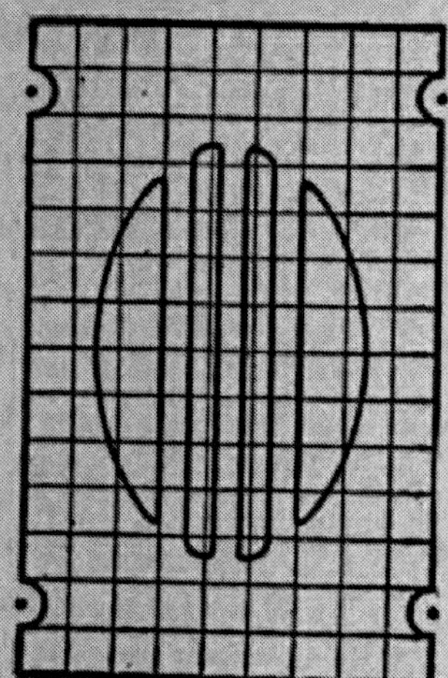

remains to make two slots in the two upper crosspieces to receive the ends of this piece, and the whole chair may be assembled. Set up with glue, secure each joint with a small peg or wire nail, and clamp until set. Small square strips should be attached to the inner surfaces of the four seat crosspieces, after which the seat-board must be accurately fitted in and secured thereto with glue and screws.

MILL BILL

PCS.	DIMENSIONS
2	1¾ x 3 x 38½
2	1¾ x 1¾ x 17½
4	⅞ x 2¾ x 15
4	⅞ x 2 x 15
2	⅞ x 2¼ x 15
1	¾ x 14 x 15
2	¼ x 6¼ x 11
1	⅜ x 9¼ x 13

BUFFET TABLE

The construction of the buffet table or sideboard should commence with the front legs, which are to be trimmed up to size, shaped on their lower ends, and finally mortised for the two crosspieces of each

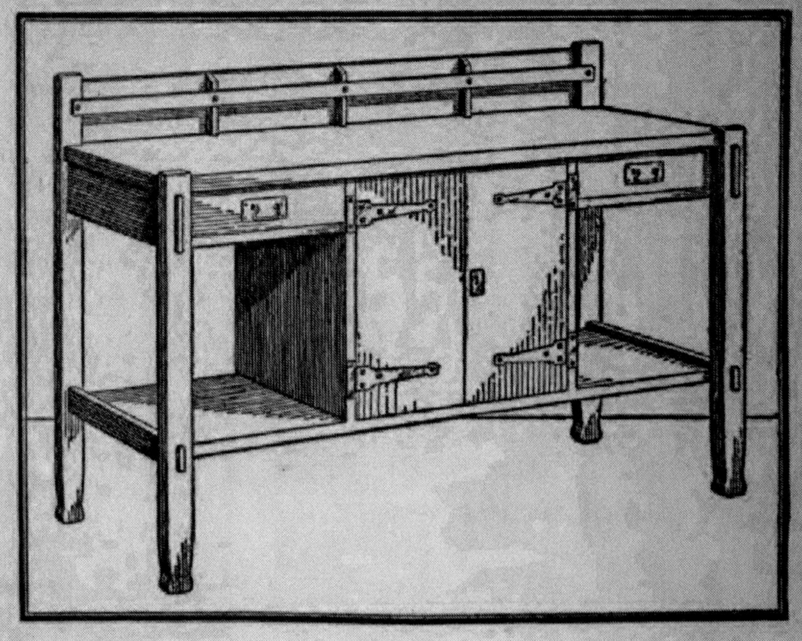

end. The rear legs are similar to the front ones in every way, except that they extend above the top board to hold the plate-rack. Having completed the legs, the two crosspieces of each end should be planed up and then tenoned to fit the mortises already made in the legs. The pieces thus far made should now be put together with glue and firmly clamped until set, taking due care to have the several

pieces all square with one another. The top board is now to be prepared. If a board of the required width cannot be found it will be necessary to glue up two smaller pieces, but in either case be sure to take particular care in finishing the upper surface and the exposed end wood.

The foot-board, which is next in order, requires nothing further than to be planed up smoothly and trimmed off perfectly square on the ends. To the inner side of each of the lower crosspieces attach a half-inch-square strip to support the foot-board. Set up the two already assembled ends and connect them with the top and foot-board, using glue and screws set in from below at an angle. A pair of temporary strips tacked on the back will keep the structure in shape as the work proceeds. The two sides of the linen compartment should now be fitted in, and then the under side of the drawer spaces. Next in order is the backing for the plate-rack, the linen compartment and drawer spaces. The linen compartment is now ready to receive the desired shelving and have its doors fitted. The hinges should be of the strap type and of a similar finish to the drawer pulls. After fitting on the several divisions of the plate-rack and attaching the running strip, the sideboard is complete, with the exception of the two drawers, the making of which will be found quite simple.

MILL BILL

PCS.	DIMENSIONS
1	1¼ x 22 x 60
1	1 x 20½ x 58
2	1¼ x 2¼ x 34
2	1¼ x 2¼ x 40
2	1 x 5 x 23
2	1 x 3 x 23
4	¾ x 11 x 21
4	¾ x 11 x 17
2	1 x 11½ x 21

PCS.	DIMENSIONS
4	½ x 11 x 15
1	½ x 6 x 57
1	⅜ x ¾ x 60

MORRIS CHAIR

The design of the Morris chair is one that will appeal to the amateur craftsman, not only on ac-

count of its unique features, but because of its simple method of construction. The illustration shows the chair with the cushions removed, in order to plainly show the construction. The cut, therefore, fails to give an adequate idea of the comfortable appearance of the chair when in use. The arm-rests at either side form the lids of two long, narrow boxes, which open outward. Many uses

will suggest themselves for these convenient little boxes. They will hold pipes and tobacco, writing materials, knitting or fancy-work, and so on.

First proceed with the ends, which are flared out at their upper ends so as to form the ends of the boxes. Each leg has but one mortise, and that through the shortest direction. After these have been prepared, the rear legs should be notched out at their upper inward corners, so that the two inner sides of the boxes can project to the rear, for the purpose of supporting the back, as shown. Four one-inch blocks of the exact size of the inside of the boxes should now be made, and fastened with screws to the upper ends of the legs, so that the sides and bottoms of the boxes may be fastened thereto. Next get out the two side crosspieces and tenon them to fit the mortises already made in the legs. The two inner sides of the boxes should now be prepared, and their ends, which project out behind, should each receive five notches, for holding the movable bar that holds the back up. After getting out the outer sides and bottoms of the boxes, the two entire sides of the chair may be assembled.

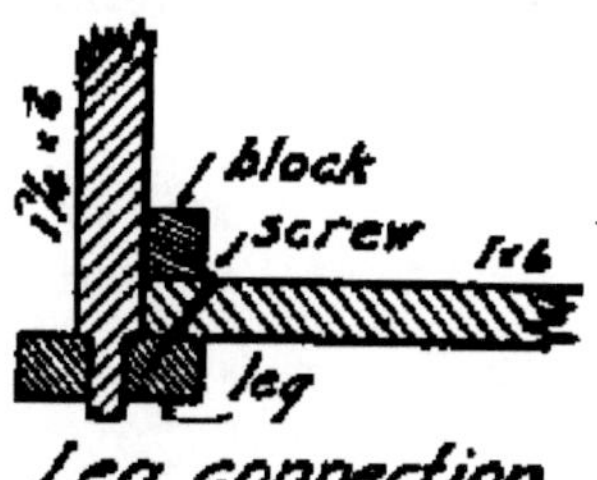

Leg connection

Use good, fresh glue, supplementing it with screws, in connecting the box pieces with the legs. The front and back crosspieces require only trimming up true and square. In the sketch is shown how to connect these to the two sides already assembled. To support the seat, five three-fourths-by-two-inch slats are nailed to two one-inch strips screwed to the inside of the two side crosspieces. The back frame consists of two tapering side pieces and five cross-bars, all of which are mortised together. These mortises are let into the side pieces of the frame for a depth of one inch, and should be set up with glue and two wire nails through each connection. To connect this frame to the back crosspiece use two stout iron hinges. The adjusting bar to regulate the angle of the back should be of hardwood or metal. The cushions may be ordered ready made in Spanish or imitation leather. If it is desired to make these at home, which is no great task, as several easily-worked materials may be used, one should first examine some of the various methods of putting these cushions together.

MILL BILL

NO. OF PIECES	DIMENSIONS
4	1¼ x 6¼ x 30
2	1¼ x 6¼ x 30
2	1 x 6¼ x 28
2	1 x 5 x 40
2	¾ x 5 x 26½
2	¾ x 6¼ x 30
2	¾ x 4½ x 26½
2	1¾ x 2 x 36
1	¾ x 3½ x 23
3	¾ x 2 x 23
1	1¼ x 3 x 23
5	¾ x 2 x 27

SMOKER'S CABINET

The cabinet shown herewith is a very convenient piece of furniture. It is a convenient stand for books and magazines and may also serve as a receptacle for smoking paraphernalia. The cabinet proper is provided with a door on either side, hinged at the bottom, so as to swing down and form a temporary shelf. A pair of brass chains should be attached to each door, in order to keep the door from dropping below the horizontal position. The four leg pieces should be first gotten out and mortised to receive the four crosspieces, and also the end panels, which are let into the sides of the legs for a depth of three-eighths of an inch. The two lower crosspieces which support the lower shelf should be tenoned at the ends to one-half by one and three-fourths inches. The upper crosspieces which support the bottom of the cabinet proper are tenoned at the ends down to one-half by one and one-half inches. Next, get out the eight little slats and cut a tenon one-fourth by one inch on each end and then mortise the crosspieces to match. After placing the slats and the crosspieces together, slip on the legs. The shelf for the bottom of the cabinet proper should now be gotten out, and after being

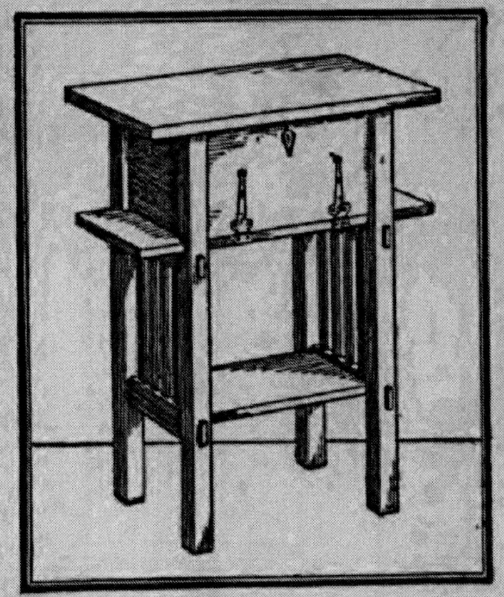

finished to the correct size, it should be very carefully notched, in order to pass around each of the four legs, beyond which it projects for a distance of three and one-half inches. If it is so desired, four holes three-fourths of an inch in diameter may be bored in each of these two projecting ends, to serve as a pipe rack. The lower shelf should now

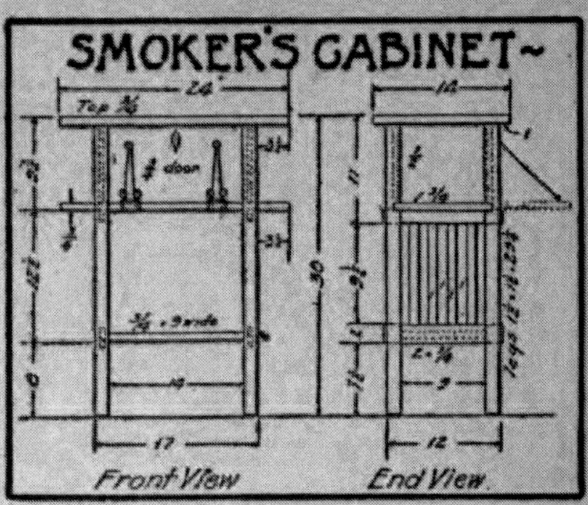

be fitted in place after taking due care to see that its length is such as to maintain the legs perfectly parallel. This shelf should be attached to the cross-pieces by means of dowel pins or with three wood screws on either end, which are screwed from the lower side of the shelf at an angle into the cross-pieces. The two doors are of three-quarter-inch lumber and each one should be provided with a pair of cross strips on the inside, to prevent warping. The top should be placed in position last, and is held

Mill Bill

PCS.	DIMENSIONS
2	2 x 2 x 42
2	2 x 2 x 32½
2	1 x 4¼ x 25½
2	1 x 4¼ x 21
2	1 x 4¼ x 45
1	1 x 4¼ x 52
1	½ x 8 x 46
2	½ x 7½ x 9
2	¼ x 8 x 8
1	½ x 9 x 45
1	¼ x 8 x 24
2	¼ x 8 x 11½
10	⅝ x 1 x 16

Also top.

SHAVING STAND

A man must have used a shaving stand in order to appreciate its many conveniences. By tilting the mirror or shifting the stand around a trifle one can always get a good light and at the same time have everything right at hand. The top receptacle is a convenient place to keep the razors, mug, strop and shaving paper, and the lower one a good place for slippers or shoe brushes.

To start the construction, the four vertical pieces should be got out and mortised to receive the side and back boards of the lower and upper receptacles. These boards should be of three-fourths-inch (the grain running horizontally), and should have a

half-inch tongue on each end to engage the corresponding mortises in the vertical pieces. The slats are three-eighths by one inch and the entire ten should be worked up together so that they will be exactly the same length. Before proceeding further it is a good plan to build up each of the two complete sides of the stand—that is, take a long and a short vertical piece, one side of each receptacle and five slats, and glue them together under pressure of clamps. The backs and bottoms of the receptacles can then be got out and the two en-

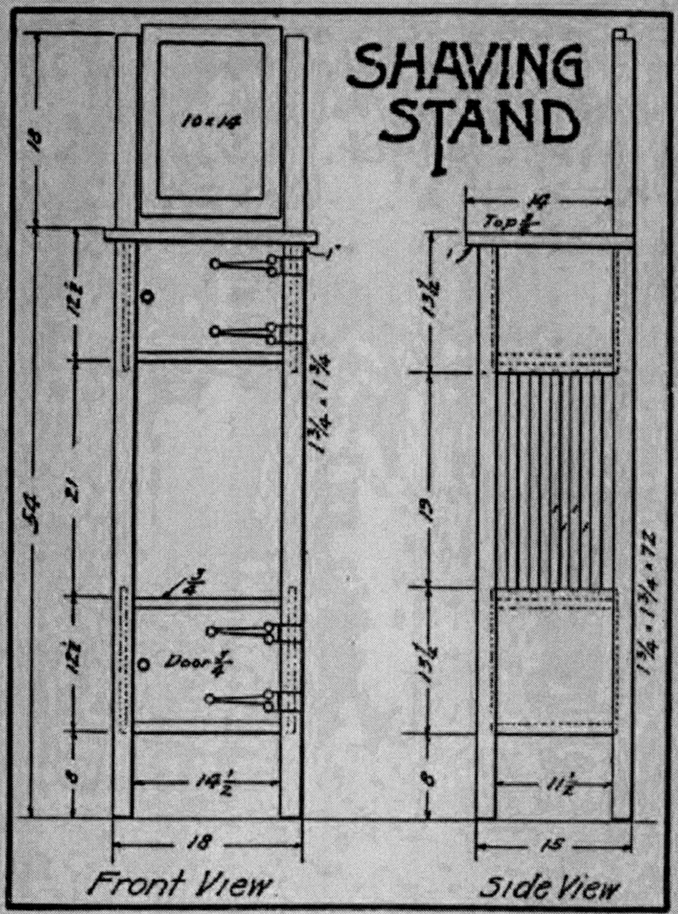

tire sides connected together, after which the top can be fastened on with glue and screws from the inside.

The doors may be made of good, clear, three-fourths-inch lumber, with the grain running horizontally, and having a pair of cleats on the back, to keep the door from warping. A more elaborate door, and possibly a better one, could be made by paneling or else by attaching a crosspiece on either end by means of glue with tongue and groove joint.

If beveled plate glass cannot be readily obtained either from stock or from some mirror already made, plain mirror glass may be bought at the hardware store, and will serve very well. The details of the frame require no explanation, as they are cut on the miter, glued together and carefully sandpapered.

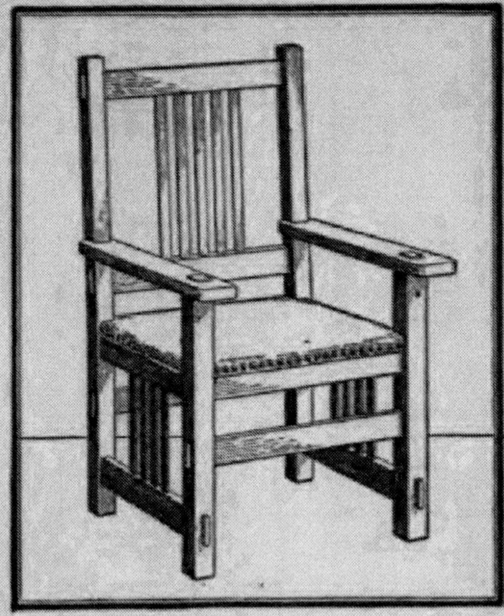

MILL BILL

NO. OF PIECES	DIMENSIONS
2	2 x 2 x 72½
2	2 x 2 x 53½
1	1 x 14½ x 20½
3	¾ x 14½ x 15½
8	1 x 2 x 15½
1	¾ x 11½ x 14½
2	½ x 9½ x 12
2	½ x 10½ x 12
10	⅜ x 1 x 19½
2	½ x 11½ x 14½

ARMCHAIR

The armchair now illustrated and the dining chair following are practically identical in construction to those previously shown, except that the panels in which the mission cross was cut are now replaced by a series of plain slats.

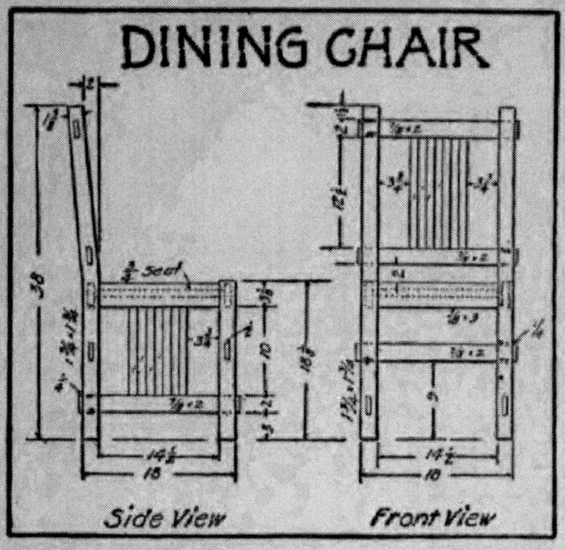

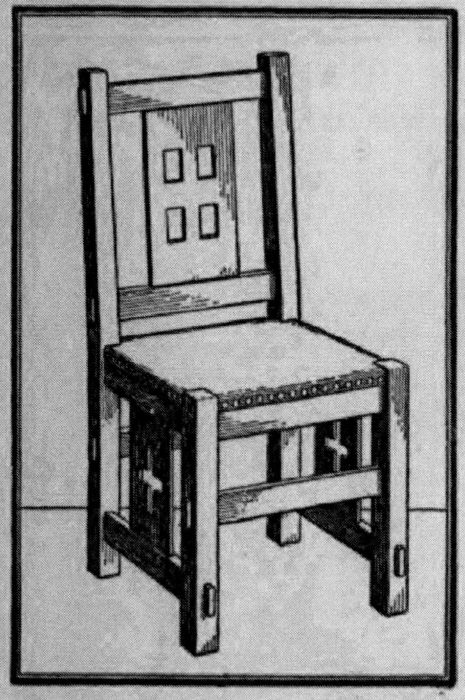

DINING CHAIR

Although originally intended for the dining room, this chair may well be used in connection with the desk illustrated a few pages back.

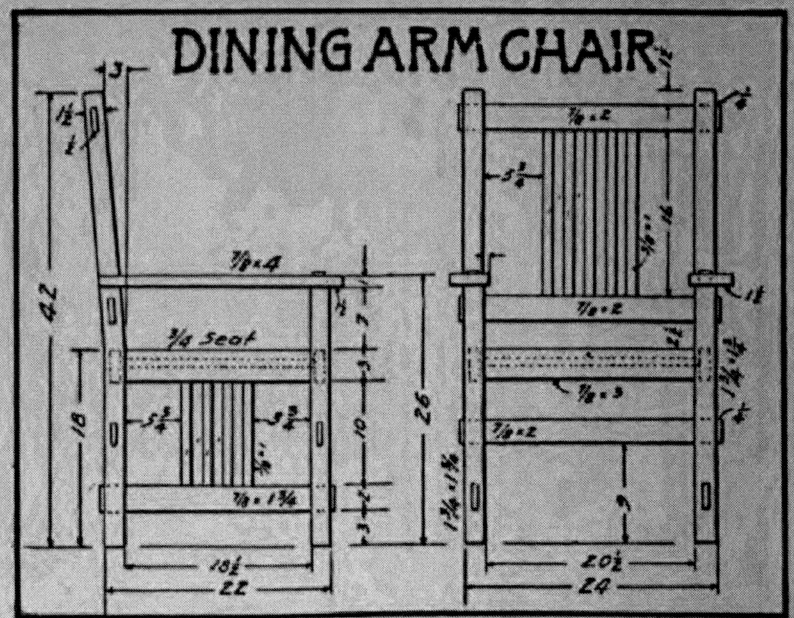

TABOURET

The similarity of this tabouret to five preceding designs will be noted.

Commence the construction with the four legs. After trimming them to a uniform length, round off the top edges slightly, and then mark off and cut the mortises for the crosspieces. These crosspieces are all tenoned to one-half by two inches. The six slats which are one-fourth by one inch need not be cut down, but should be let into the crosspieces full size for a distance of three-eighths of an inch. The two sides should be set up complete with glue, and clamped until dry, after which the remaining slats and crosspieces may be placed in position and glued. The top should be carefully notched, so as to pass neatly around the leg pieces, and then fastened by screws to the top crosspieces. These screws should be put in from underneath and at an angle through the crosspieces. Should pine be used for the construction, an exception should be made in the wood for the slender side slats, and hard wood used instead.

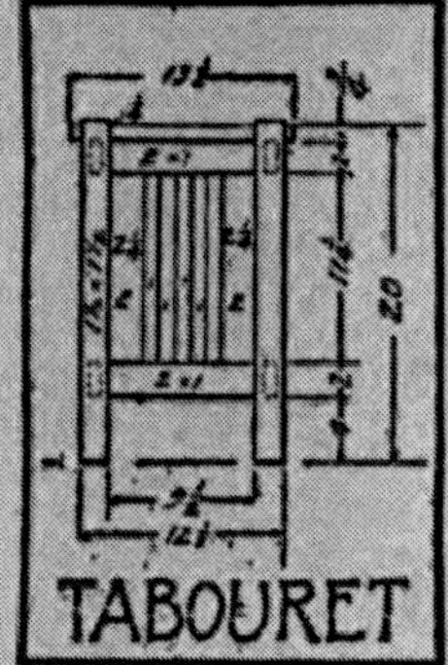

MILL BILL

NO. OF PIECES	DIMENSIONS
4	1¾ x 1¾ x 20¼
8	1 x 2 x 10½
1	¾ x 13¾ x 13¾
6	¼ x 1 x 12

BOOK RACK

It was with the family living-room in mind that the design for the book rack was made. The lower two shelves will each hold a row of books on either side, the next will keep the current magazines in

order, while the top space may be similarly used or else assigned to the exclusive use of the unabridged dictionary. The two small overhanging shelves are convenient for little books and pamphlets.

In the construction of this piece much will depend on the accuracy with which the ends of the shelves and side pieces are finished to the required angle. This angle, however, is constant throughout, and when once the gauge is set to the proper reading a little care and patience will accomplish the rest.

Commence with the sides. If the lumber available does not glue up wide enough to get out the small projections at the feet, simply glue on a small block at each corner. Mark out the entire outline, positions of the shelves, dowel-pin holes, and the ornamental openings, then proceed to work carefully down to these lines, having in mind all the while the necessity of obtaining a good clear outline at whatever angle the piece is viewed.

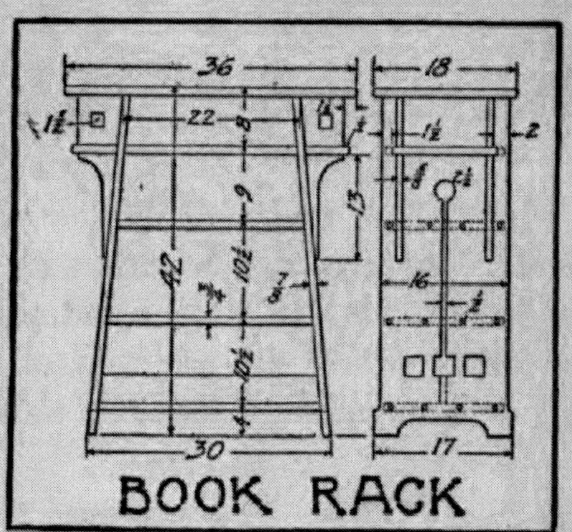

The bottom and the top shelf are the first to be made ready and should be fitted to sides with dowel pins temporarily placed before the exact lengths of the two intermediate shelves can be determined.

When these latter and the top have been made ready, the assembling may commence.

Give all the end wood a preliminary coat of glue as a filler and when this is dry put the structure together. If the ordinary long clamps are not available, provide some way of wedging the sides together until the glue sets. Later attach the top with screws set in from below at an angle, after which make ready the side shelves and brackets. Attach each bracket with glue and brads set in from the inside. Glue and nail the shelves to these, after which the addition of the small end boards will completely hide the nails.

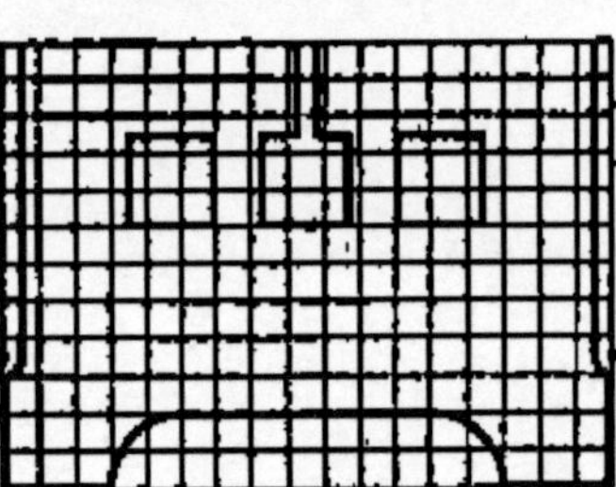

MILL BILL

PCS.	DIMENSIONS
1	⅞ x 17 x 42
1	¾ x 15½ x 28
1	¾ x 15½ x 36
1	¾ x 15½ x 24
1	¾ x 15½ x 22
2	¾ x 6 x 14
2	⅞ x 17 x 42
4	⅝ x 6 x 7
4	⅝ x 5¼ x 13½

MORRIS CHAIR

The illustration of the Morris chair does not give any adequate idea of its roomy comfort, since the two large cushions are not shown. The arm-rests are quite low and very wide, thus providing ample space for a book or writing-paper. The angle of

the back is easily adjusted by moving two loosely-fitting pegs, which are set into holes bored in the rearward projecting ends of the arm-rests.

The making of this chair should commence with

the four legs, which are all of a length and similarly cut down on their upper ends so as to pass through and support the arm-rests. The long, narrow mortises for the crosspieces should be very accurately marked off and cut from both sides with a sharp

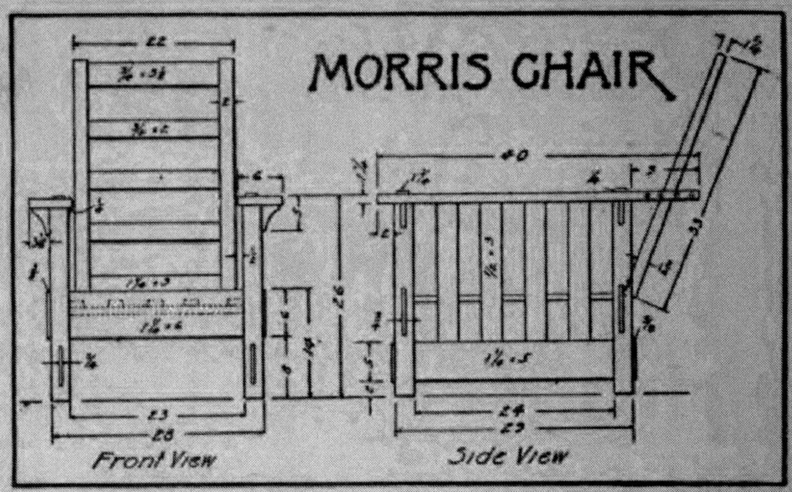

chisel. Next proceed with the arm-rests, cutting the two square holes in each, and then bore the eight holes for the adjusting pegs. The two side crosspieces are now in order, and must be carefully tenoned to fit the mortises already made in the legs. On the under side of the arm-rests and on the upper edges of these crosspieces cut the mortises for the side slats, which should then be gotten out and tenoned to a uniform length. We are now ready to assemble the two entire sides of our chair, which should be set up with glue and firmly clamped for about eight hours. The front and back crosspieces may now be gotten out, and the two sides connected. The back frame consists of two slightly-tapering side pieces and five cross-bars tenoned into the side pieces for a depth of one inch. Set up with glue, and through each connection drive a couple of wire nails with the heads carefully set. Attach this frame to the back crosspiece with two stout hinges. To support the seat-cushions, two-by-three-fourths-inch slats should be arranged as shown. These slats rest on two one-inch-square strips which are screwed to the inside of the front and back crosspieces. The cushions may be ordered already made, or they may be made at home from one of the several available materials. There are several methods of sewing up a cushion for such a chair as this, but as this is hardly within the scope of this article, the writer would suggest that those who have had no experience in this line examine some cushions at the furniture-store.

MILL BILL

NO. OF PIECES	DIMENSIONS
4	2½ x 2½ x 27
2	1¼ x 6¼ x 29½
2	1¼ x 5¼ x 30½
2	1¼ x 6¼ x 40½
2	1¾ x 2 x 33½
1	¾ x 3½ x 21
8	¾ x 2 x 21
1	1¼ x 3 x 21

NO. OF PIECES	DIMENSIONS
8	½ x 3 x 19
5	¾ x 2 x 26
2	1 x 1 x 24

SETTEE

The loose cushion has so many advantages over the regular form of upholstering that it has become very popular in recent years. A settee or chair provided with loose cushions may be arranged so as to be comfortable for almost any position the occupant may assume, and has the further advantage that it can always be easily and thoroughly cleaned. These cushions may be made from a variety of materials such as Spanish leather, pantosote, velour, burlap, etc., and are quite attractive in appearance. But a slight idea of the comfort of this piece of furniture can be had from the cut, as the settee is shown completely bare.

The following is the preferable order of preparing the various pieces: Start with the corner posts. After squaring up to the proper length—giving special care to the tops—mark out the location of the mortises. It will be noted on the drawing that the cross-bar tenons extend slightly beyond the corner posts. Those of the front and the two back-rails extend into the posts for one and one-quarter inches. In forming the feet make a saw cut for a depth of three eighths of an inch on the four sides,

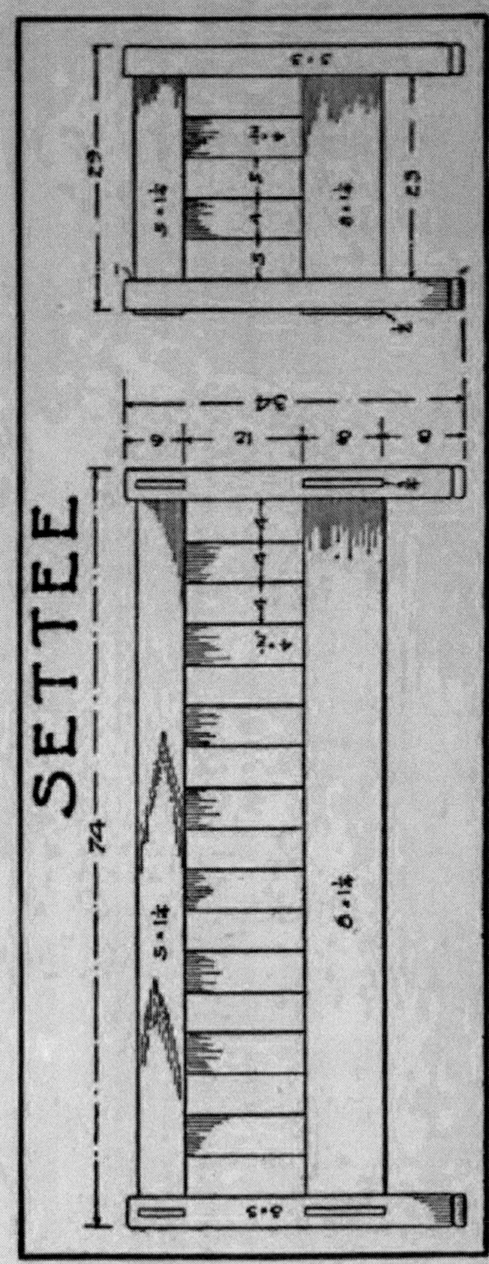

and then finish with the chisel. Having completed the corner posts take up the cross-bars for each and fit them to the posts, which operation will probably require more care than any other in the construction. Next prepare the front and two back-rails, fitting them to the corner posts as already mortised. The grooves for the four end and eight back boards must now be cut in the cross-bars and back-rails, and the twelve boards fitted thereto. The putting together may now be proceeded with. Connect the corner posts of each end with the cross-bars, using glue at all joints. The two ends thus formed may then be set up and connected by the front and two back rails (with the eight back boards in position, of course). Should there be any question as to the stiffness of the joints of the corner posts with the rails and cross-bars each corner should be reënforced with a large block firmly secured with glue and nails. When the seat is in position these blocks will not be seen. To hold the seat boards up nail strips on the inner sides of the rails and cross-bars, so set that the seat line will fall about a half inch below the top of the rails. This slight depression keeps the cushions in place. For the seat, or back, one long cushion, or three shorter ones, may be provided. These must be firmly filled and be of uniform thickness all over.

MILL BILL

POS.	DIMENSIONS
4	3 x 3 x 35
2	1¼ x 8¼ x 71
1	1¼ x 5¼ x 71
2	1¼ x 8¼ x 30
2	1¼ x 5¼ x 30
12	½ x 4¼ x 13
9	⅝ x 8 x 26

PORCH SWING

The framework of the swing is largely of two-by-four pine. Smooth up the two long runners and

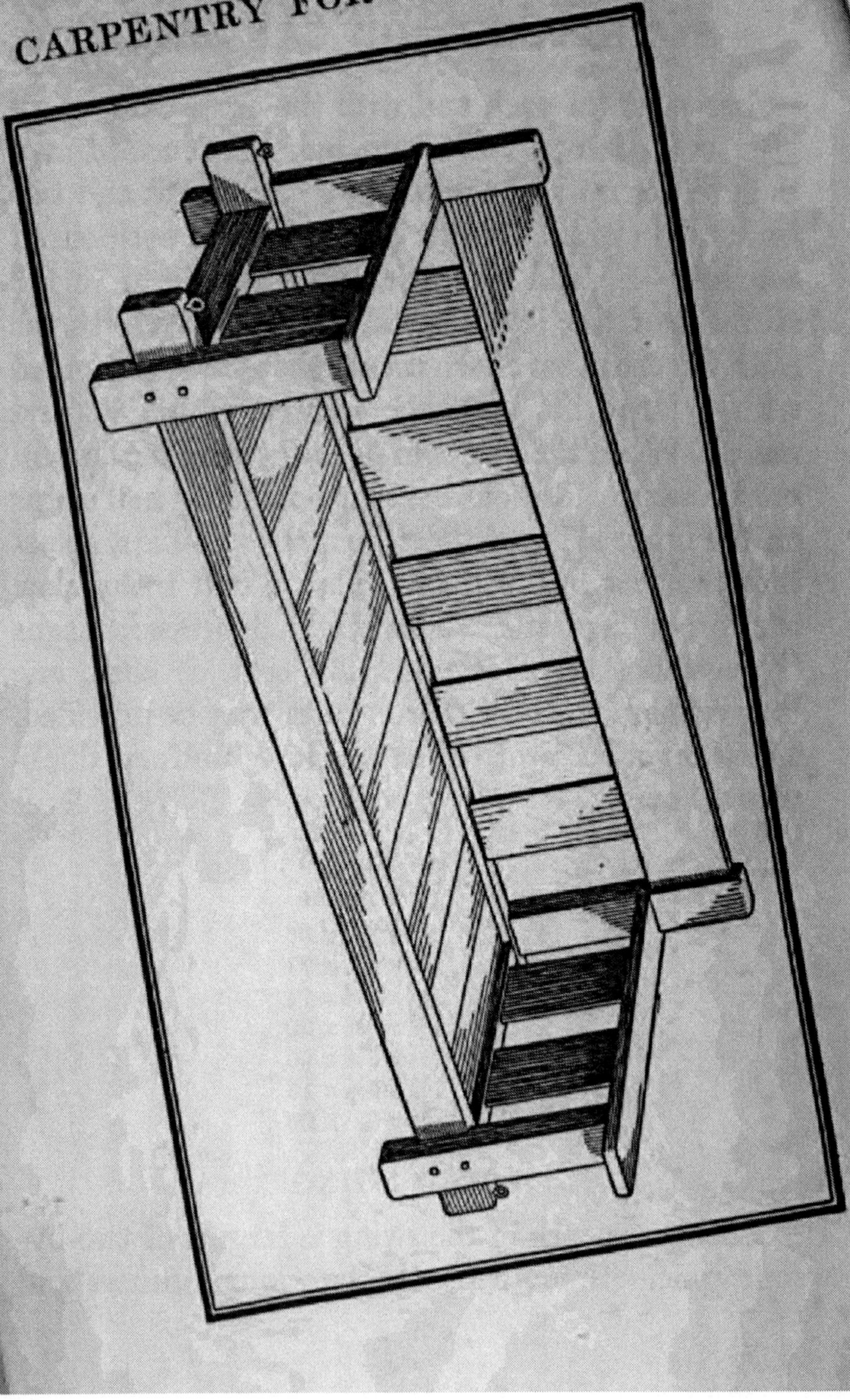

round the ends slightly. Prepare the two cross-bars, making the ends perfectly flat and square. Towards the lower end of each of the four corner posts a section is cut out so that the long runners will set in half an inch, as shown in the end view drawing. Mortises, three-fourths of an inch wide and one and one-quarter inches deep, should then be cut for the back rail.

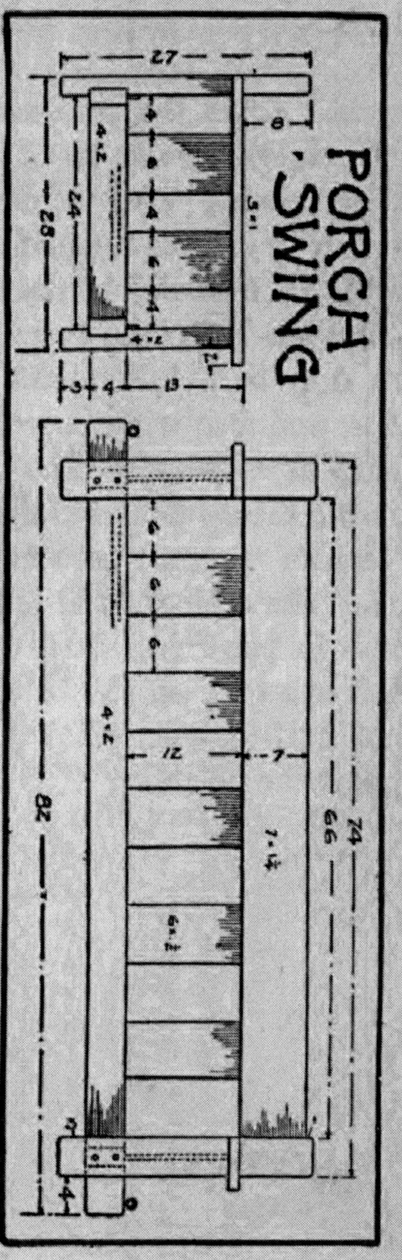

The pieces may now be put together. At each corner a pair of lag-screws are inserted through the corner post and runner into the cross-bar. Three-eighths-inch screws, with a washer under the head, are used. Grooves can now be cut for the five back and four end boards. After the back rail is prepared and similarly grooved, tenon to fit the mortises in the rear corner posts. The arm-rests should now be grooved to receive the end boards. After preparing the nine small boards, and fitting them to the grooves made to hold them, the back rail and arm-rests may be put in place. Use glue at all these joints, and also wire nails driven in from below or behind as required. The connection of the runners and cross-bars should be reënforced by a block in each of the four corners secured with nails and glue. These blocks will not be seen when the bottom is in position. Strips nailed on the inside of the framework set so that the seat-line will fall about half an inch below the top of the runners, support the bottom.

MILL BILL

PCS.	DIMENSIONS
2	2 x 4 x 33
2	2 x 4 x 27½
2	2 x 4 x 20
2	2 x 4 x 22
1	1¼ x 7¼ x 70
2	1 x 5 x 31
9	½ x 6 x 13
8	¾ x 8 x 22

CHAPTER 4

WHITE ENAMEL FURNITURE

White enameled furniture is not only peculiarly appropriate for the bedroom, but is well adapted to home construction, inasmuch as soft and inexpensive woods may be used and any slight defects in the wood or in the fitting may be puttied over. The use of putty further simplifies the construction by making it possible to use nails wherever desired. Those who have not seen new wood properly treated and coated with white or cream enamel rubbed to a flat finish after the modern fashion cannot fully appreciate the very fine effect.

Another possibility with this finish is that a stripe, or even a light stencil design, of the prevailing tint of the bedroom, may be run around the fronts of the drawers, a good deal after the fashion of the inlaid strips with which Sheraton embellished his lovely furniture. The reader will of course understand that the white enamel finish is not impera-

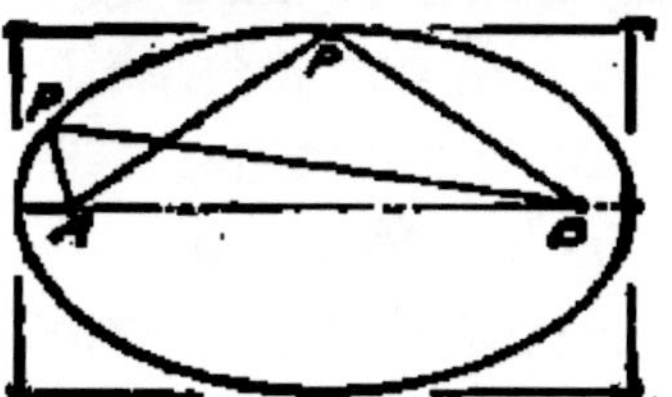

tive, but if stains are used, a light effect [illegible] for such large surfaces.

The appearance of these pieces will [illegible] measure depend on the accuracy with [illegible] curves around the feet are worked out. [illegible] curves are all elliptical, and an ellipse is [illegible] as easy to lay out as a circle if gone about [illegible] right way. In the working drawings [illegible] small diagram which shows how to lay [illegible] accurate ellipse. Suppose that a string [illegible] from a tack at A, around a pencil-point (P) [illegible] tack at B. Then any movement of the pencil [illegible] keeps the string tight will trace a perfect ellipse. The distance between the points A and B are [illegible] and three-fourths inches for the seat, ten and three-eighths for wash-stand, eleven for bedside-stand, and twelve and five-eighths for dresser.

In sawing out these curves with the key hole-saw, proceed slowly, so as to avoid tearing up splinters along the outside. The finishing down to line will require the use of the spoke-shave and considerable sandpaper. The very simplicity of the outline will necessitate a sharp edge in order to be effective.

In the matter of painting and enameling you can spend about as much or as little time as you care to, depending on the results desired. After thoroughly wiping off the sandpaper-dust, touch up any sappy spots or knots with shellac, and then fill any defects with putty, which, by the way, should never be applied to new wood without having first oiled the place to be puttied.

The first coat should be of good white paint (white lead, linseed-oil, and turpentine), which should be lightly sanded when dry and then receive a second coat. By this time our piece of furniture will begin to look quite well. The better enamels usually are accompanied by a preliminary "undercoat" preparation, which should follow the white paint, and is sometimes applied in as many as three or four coats, between each of which the piece is thoroughly rubbed. The finishing-coat is of the enamel proper, and may be left with the gloss or rubbed flat.

The result of all this labor is a beautiful smooth surface that will wear for years. A quite satisfactory finish, however, may be obtained with a coat of white paint, followed by one of prepared enamel. In fact, a good smooth surface treated in this way will be superior to a rougher one receiving the more elaborate finish.

Many of the pieces in this set will have to be glued up from two or more pieces of wood, a feature of the work that may be conveniently attended to at the mill.

There is really nothing to prevent the homeworker from making a bedroom-set of this sort, provided he will work carefully, slowly, and with accuracy. It will be necessary for him to have good tools, and a reliable square is absolutely essential. Without careful measurements and a thorough "truing up" of joints and corners, the work will have a very amateurish look which no amount of painting and enameling can rectify. All of the tools used in making furniture should be of good quality, sharp and in the best condition. No great amount of skill or experience is needed by the workman, but he does need patience, and must be painstaking.

Although this bedroom-set is to be finished in white enamel, it would be quite possible to finish it in the light French-gray enamel which is now so popular. This enamel is copied from some of the old French enameled furniture, and is very beautiful. Another suggestion for finishing is to decorate the set, after it has been finished in white enamel, with small medallions in Wedgewood blue with white figures. These would necessarily have to be copied from good designs in a first-class furniture establishment. This, too, is a very new idea and very beautiful when successfully done.

However, these are merely suggestions. If the set is well made and finished in white or ivory enamel without any decorations, it will be found to be very handsome and satisfactory to the most fas-

The curved back strip and the two uprights that support the mirror are next in order; and, after mortising them together, secure them to the top by glue and by nails set in from below through the

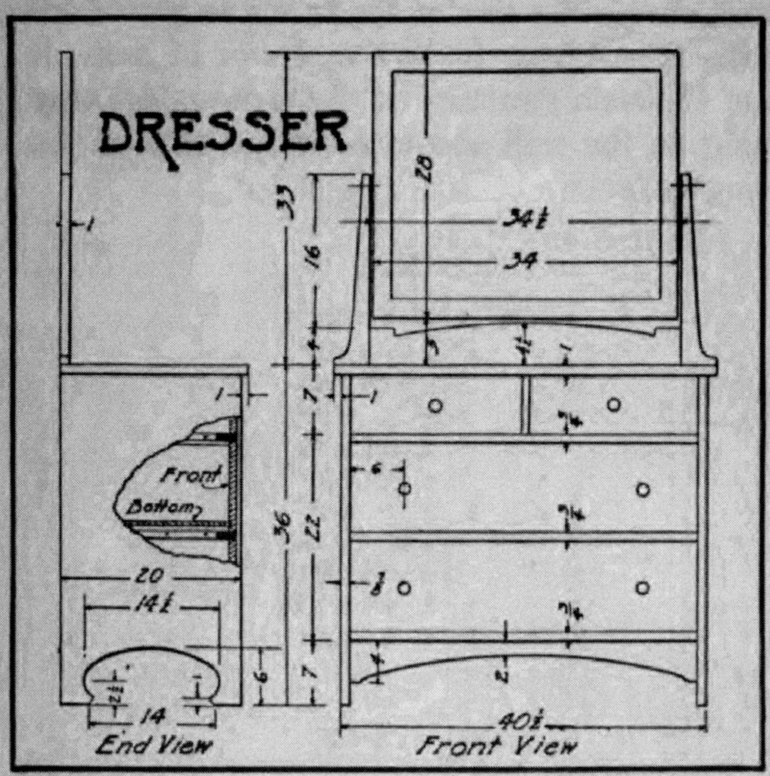

top board. The back should now be closed and the curved foot strip shaped up and secured in place, after which the drawers will receive our attention. A moment's inspection of any well-made piece of furniture will clearly indicate the best and most workmanlike manner of connecting the several thin pieces of wood that form the inner portion of the dresser-drawer.

Beveled plate is desirable for the mirror, and if a piece of almost the correct size can be reasonably secured, change the size of the frame to accommodate it. The mirror feature need not be made a part of the main structure of the dresser, but may be hung on the wall above, as in the case of the dressing-table.

Mill Bill

PCS.	DIMENSIONS
1	1 x 21½ x 48
2	⅞ x 20½ x 36
3	¾ x 3 x 39½
1	¾ x 6½ x 20
1	¾ x 4¼ x 39½
6	1 x 1 x 17
2	¾ x 11 x 39½
2	¾ x 6½ x 20
2	1 x 4½ x 20½
1	1 x 5 x 35

WASH-STAND

The general method of constructing the wash-stand is similar to that of the dresser. The two sides are first to be made ready in the manner previously described, after which the bottom board and top are to be trimmed up true and square. Assemble these four pieces, and then nail two temporary, diagonal strips across the back to stiffen the structure as the work proceeds.

The piece upon which the top drawer rests is now to be fitted and secured in place, after which put in the vertical division. Shape up and attach the curved strip below the bottom board. The curved back strip, the two uprights, and the towel-rack should all be fitted together before placing on the top, to which they are attached by nailing from below.

After closing in the back, it only remains to fit on the door and to make the three drawers. If desired, the two smaller drawers may be omitted and a door substituted, thus simplifying the construction somewhat.

MILL BILL

PCS.	DIMENSIONS
1	1 x 19½ x 33
2	⅞ x 18½ x 30
2	¾ x 18 x 29
2	¾ x 1 x 18

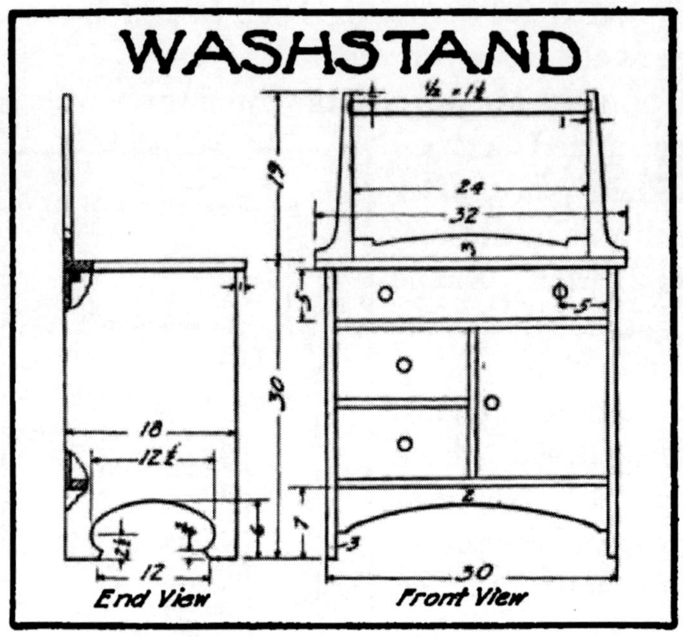

PCS.	DIMENSIONS
1	¾ x 18 x 16
1	¾ x 3 x 15
1	¾ x 5¼ x 29
2	¾ x 8 x 15
1	¾ x 15 x 16
1	¾ x 4¼ x 29
1	¾ x 3 x 25
2	1 x 4¼ x 19½
1	½ x 1½ x 27

BEDSIDE-STAND

Accurately draw out the shape of the two sides directly upon the wood, and then saw them, all as previously described. Squarely trim up the three cross boards, mark their positions on the sides, and

then secure them in position, using glue and screws or nails according to whether the piece is to be stained or enameled. The top is now in order, and after finishing the end wood flat and smooth, secure it in place. Neatly fill in the back of the drawer-space and the lower compartment, which is then ready to have its door fitted.

If the wood shows any tendency to warp, or is not thoroughly dry, fasten two cross cleats to the back.

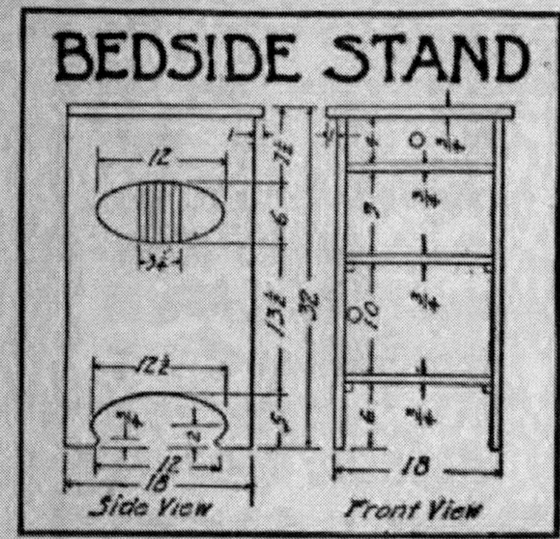

The making and fitting of the drawers in the usual manner will now require attention, after which the three small slats in the elliptical opening of each side are to be placed. As mortises are here impractical, see that these slats fit tightly, and then apply at each end some glue and a strong wire nail driven in from the inside at the proper angle.

MILL BILL

PCS.	DIMENSIONS
1	¾ x 19¼ x 20½
3	¾ x 17 x 18
2	⅞ x 18½ x 32
1	¾ x 4¼ x 17
1	¾ x 10¼ x 17

DRESSING-TABLE

As usual, the two sides are first in order, after which the board that supports the shelf and the foot-rail are to be trimmed up to their respective widths and to the same length. As soon as the top has been made ready, the two sides are to be set up and connected. On account of the direction of the grain in that portion of each side just below the elliptical openings, care should be taken not to hammer so vigorously as to split the wood.

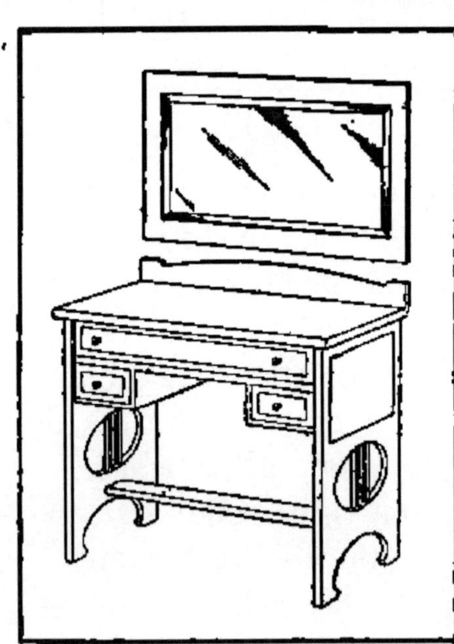

The sides and bottoms of the spaces for the two smaller drawers are now to be made ready and glued and nailed in place. The curved back strip on top is now to be gotten out and attached. Fill in the back of the three drawer-spaces, and then

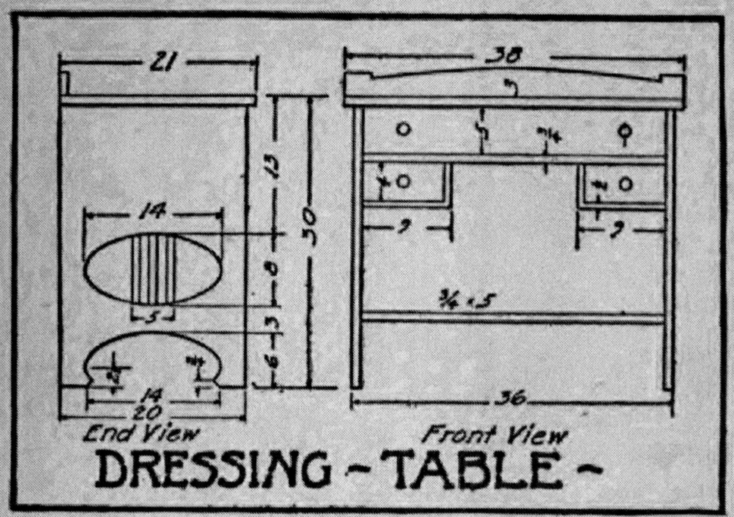

snugly fit in the three slats in each end opening, securing each slat with glue and a wire nail at each end. It now only remains to make and fit the drawers—and our table is complete.

Mill Bill

PCS.	DIMENSIONS
1	1 x 21½ x 38½
2	⅞ x 20½ x 30
1	¾ x 20 x 35
1	¾ x 3¼ x 38½
2	¾ x 5¼ x 35
2	½ x 9 x 20
2	½ x 4¾ x 20

DRESSING-TABLE SEAT

This little seat so closely resembles the table just described that little need be said as to its construction. A back on a dressing-table chair is a nuisance, and the short backs often placed on them give the chair a deformed appearance, and are necessarily too low to add anything to the comfort.

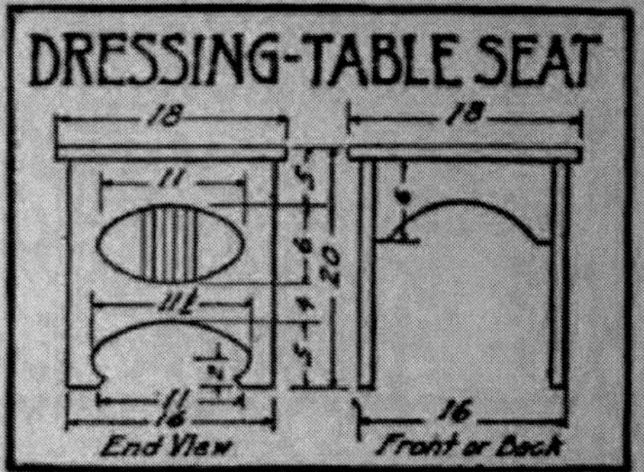

Aside from the small slats in the oval openings, five pieces are all that are needed for this little seat. The two curved strips are first secured to the under side of the seat, and then the ends are fastened to both.

Mill Bill

PCS.	DIMENSIONS
1	7/8 x 18½ x 18½
2	7/8 x 16½ x 20
2	7/8 x 6¼ x 15

CHAPTER 5

Lamps for the Home

The following lamp designs are presented not so much on account of the merit of the particular lamps described, but rather to acquaint the reader with the general method of construction and to draw attention to the possibilities of home carpentry along this line. There is probably no field more interesting to the home craftsman than the making of lamps as the final result is almost always delightfully surprising. This is largely due to the fact that so many excellent accessories may be purchased at the stores, and an endless variety is possible in the way of shades. Thus, wire forms of every desirable shape can be had at a slight cost, and any one handy with the needle can produce a beautiful silk shade.

Then again, those who have no electric current available may secure a great variety of oil burners. The "oil candle" is simply a burner mounted on a metal oil container, which, on account of its tubular form, may readily be concealed in the woodwork of the lamp. A ring is usually provided at the top so that the shade may be conveniently supported. Other and larger burners may be had with copper oil pots that may to good advantage be worked into such lamps as the library lamp to be described a little later.

Corresponding to the "oil candle" there has lately come on the market an electric socket operated by a pull chain and adapted to slip into a candle holder. As the flexible conducting cord passes out at the side of the socket no wiring is necessary. This fixture alone makes possible a great variety of effects to the amateur craftsman.

CANDLE SCONCE

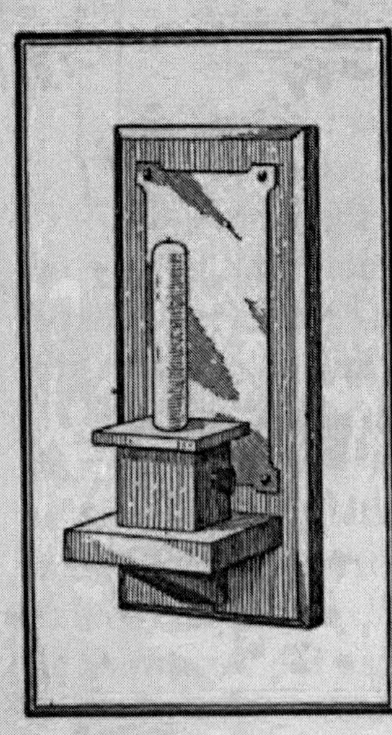

In the electric candle sconce illustrated an ordinary key socket, such as is used on drop lights, is neatly boxed in with the key projecting from one side. The box is then mounted on a small shelf in front of a piece of polished brass or copper to serve as a reflector. When the woodwork is neatly finished and a frosted candle-shaped electric lamp is used, the effect is very quaint and attractive. Such a fixture is inexpensive and makes an excellent hall light or side light in the dining room or on each side of the dresser.

The back board is first to be prepared. Square up the ends and smooth off the end wood. Mark the guide lines for the bevel edges, and then plane them off, taking due care not to tear off splinters at the corners when planing crossways. The shelf will next be shaped up, after which bore a half-inch hole clear through at the center so that the end of the socket will set in. Fasten the shelf to the back with two screws set in from behind, and then prepare the small bracket underneath, which is to be fastened in place with glue and a few nails driven in from behind and down through the shelf, taking care in the latter case to so place the nails that the box will finally hide them. A box two inches square will then be made of one-quarter inch material so as to inclose the socket. A quarter-inch slot will then be made in the center of one side so that the box may be slipped down over the key of the

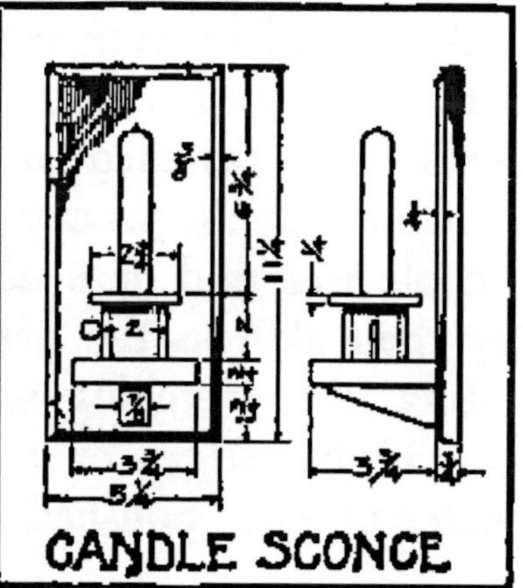
CANDLE SCONCE

socket. Bore a five-sixteenth inch hole through the back and into the shelf connecting with the hole already made through the shelf at the center. Connect the wires to the socket, and run them out through this hole to the back. Place the small box over the socket and secure it in place, and then close up the slot in the side below the key by fitting and gluing in a small piece of wood. The top of the box is now in order, and besides being finished up smoothly with square edges and corners, should receive a large hole in the center, so that the candle-lamp may be screwed into the socket. When this is fastened in place the woodwork is complete and ready for finishing.

A piece of brass or copper large enough to form a reflector should then be secured, shaped up as desired and fastened to the back. Those who are familiar with the process of etching as taught in the schools will find here an excellent opportunity to try their skill as the plate may be rendered quite decorative by etching some simple, formal design around the edges or at the corners, leaving the center brightly polished and lacquered.

PORCH OR HALL LANTERN

In constructing a hall or porch lantern special attention must be given to the matter of ventilation if the source of illumination is to be kerosene, otherwise the lamp will smoke and overheat the lantern. This feature is taken care of in the accompanying design by boring several holes in the bottom, about five more under each eave, and by provid-

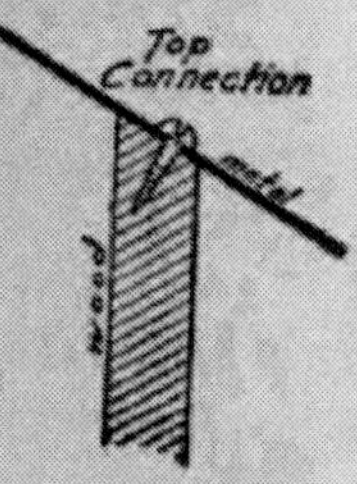

ing four triangular covered openings in the top, which is to be made of galvanized iron or of heavy tin, painted a dull black.

This metal work need not cause any one to hesitate, for no greater difficulty is involved than that of placing a few rivets. The four triangular faces of the top are in one piece, which is to be cut according to the dimensions given in the pattern drawing and then bent along the dotted lines. The four vent holes are then cut, and holes drilled for the rivets that join the first and last sections. The four small pointed roofs over these vents are then cut according to the dimensions given, properly shaped

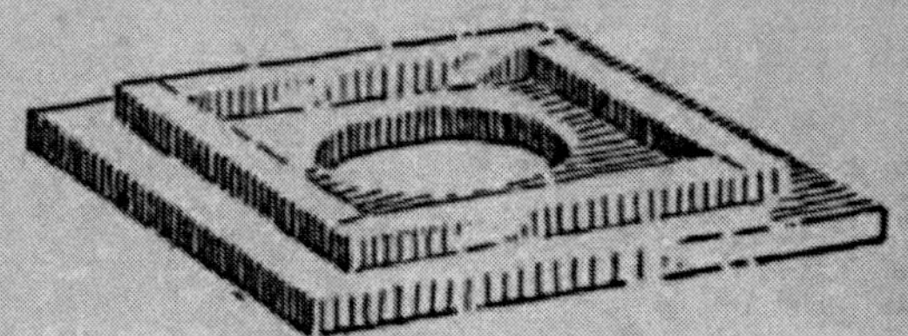

and riveted in place. After making a ring from heavy copper wire with flattened ends and riveting

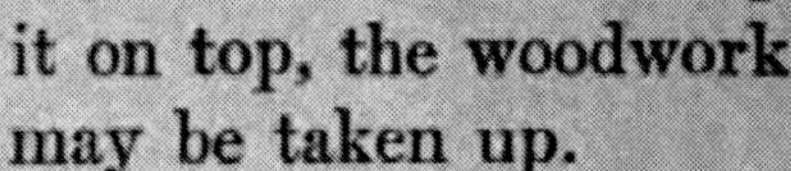

it on top, the woodwork may be taken up.

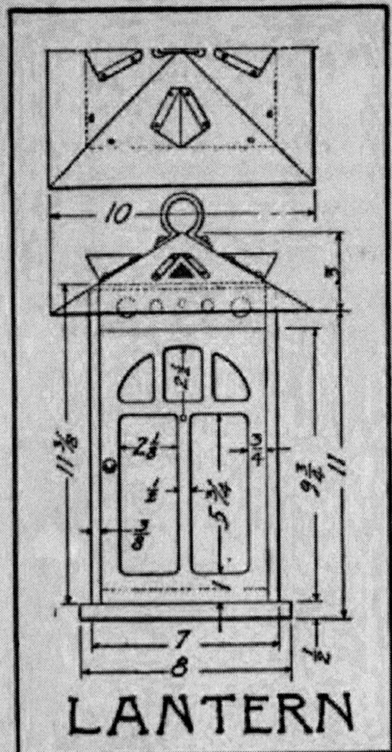

Three sides of the lantern are each made from a single piece, whereas the fourth side is in two pieces, the lower one of which forms the door, which extends from the base upward as high as the over-hanging top will permit. Before cutting the openings for the glass, fit all these pieces together and see that the upper edges are all cut off at an angle that corresponds with the slope of the top. Lay out the pattern for the side openings, and after transferring it to the wood, proceed with the sawing. Finish all edges accurately and smoothly, and bore the vent holes near the top.

Now prepare the bottom, and after trimming it up squarely to size, fasten four half-inch strips to the upper side, so that the three sides of the lantern may be the more easily connected and the door kept from swinging inside. All these pieces may be put together, after which the top will be secured with about eight screws set in as shown in the small sketch. The placing of the glass on the inside is now in order, after which the door should be hinged in place and provided with some simple clasp or knob. A coat of very dark stain to the wood and of drop black to the top serve to complete the lantern.

A suitable lamp may usually be found in the department stores for a small price. If electricity is available, it is a very simple matter to hang a small globe inside. The lantern may then be hung directly on the cord, or if a chain is used the wires should be intertwined with the links.

DESK LAMP

In considering the advisability of making the desk lamp shown in the accompanying illustration the reader need not hesitate on account of the metal work involved in the construction of the shade. This should not hinder the undertaking, however, as it is possible to get almost any sort of a shade at the

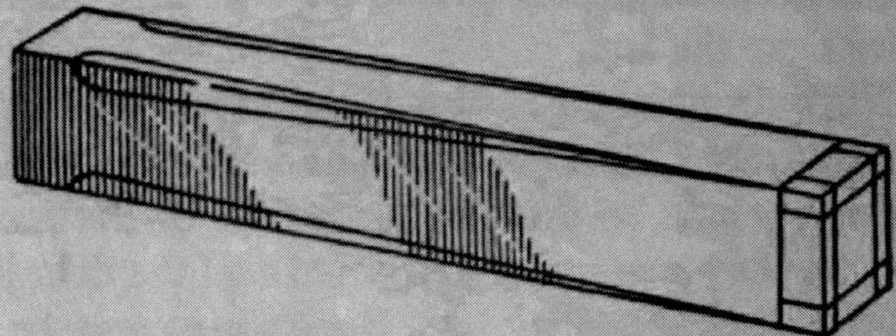

department stores, after which the lamp may be constructed to match.

The standard will constitute the chief care. Select a piece of straight-grained material an inch and a half square and of the requisite length. With a sharp pencil mark off the various lines as indicated in the detail drawing. Cut down one side to line and then the side opposite, after which mark the lines for cutting the other two sides, and then work them down. Proceed slowly and carefully, testing with the try-square frequently as the work advances. When the final surfaces have been secured, but not before, bevel off the four corners. The lower end is now to be reduced to one inch square to fit into the base, and a three-eighth inch hole is to be bored clear through the center. The base block will be next in order. Do not attempt to bevel off the edges until the piece has been smoothed off squarely and to the exact size. Accurately lay out the necessary lines on the sides and top before proceeding to cut away the extra material. When finished bore a hole through the center

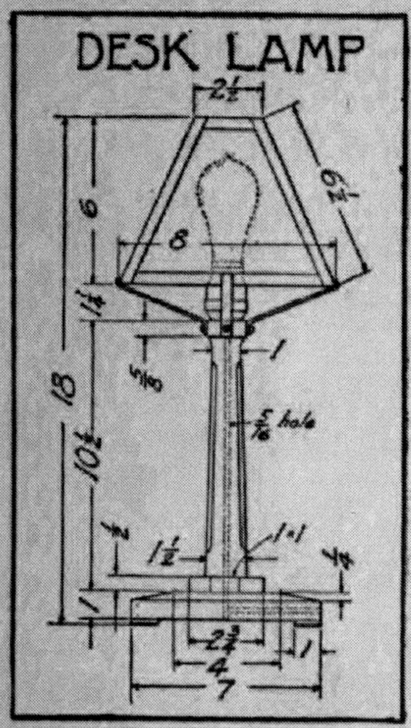

the same size as the one in the standard and another in through one side about the size of a lead pencil to connect therewith. At each corner on the underside glue on a small block one inch square and a quarter of an inch thick. The block on top of the base is next to be prepared with a square hole in the center to match the bottom of the standard. Fasten this piece to the base with glue and a few nails driven in through the base from below, after which glue the standard in position, clamping it firmly overnight.

The staining and polishing is now in order, after which run in the flexible conducting cord and connect the socket. A simple way to hold this in position is to procure a piece of brass tubing about two inches long and thread or solder it into the end of the socket. Slightly enlarge the hole in the top of the standard so that this tube may be snugly forced in without splitting the wood, and the socket will be securely held in an upright position. The four brackets that support the shade may be made from narrow strips of brass, or from stout wire, bent as indicated and fastened with round-headed screws to the top of the standard.

WALL FIXTURE

With the present design a simple method of connecting shades to ordinary key sockets is introduced that will undoubtedly appeal to the amateur craftsman. A hole is cut in the top of the shade large enough for the end of the socket to pass through. Four strips of stiff tin, about a quarter of an inch wide by an inch long, are firmly bound or soldered around the socket, which is then slipped through the hole in the top of the shade. The strips of tin are spread outward so as to support the shade, all as set forth in the accompanying sectional sketch, A small screw or tack in each piece of tin will prevent the shade from rotating on the socket.

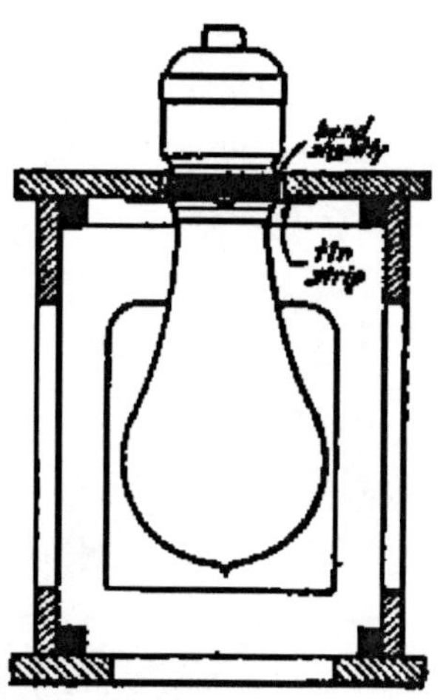

The top and bottom pieces of the shade are first to be made ready, and after the holes have been sawed out and made smooth, nail some small strips around the under side of each top piece and around the top side of each bottom piece, in the case of the hall lantern. The eight side panels are now in order, and will be worked out with the scroll saw as usual. When all edges have been made smooth and square, arrange for holding the colored or frosted glass securely in place. If suitable glass cannot be obtained, use heavy colored paper. The pieces may now be put together with a few very fine wire brads and glue.

In the meantime proceed with the wall bracket.

The central arm will be made as in the detail view, tenoned on one end, pointed at the other, and notched out to hold the crossbar that supports the shades. This latter piece will also be pointed and similarly notched. When these two pieces have been fitted neatly and squarely together, drill two holes for the ends of the sockets to fit in and two smaller ones clear through for the wires, which are carried along through grooves to the central arm, where they join and pass to the back. The two wall blocks

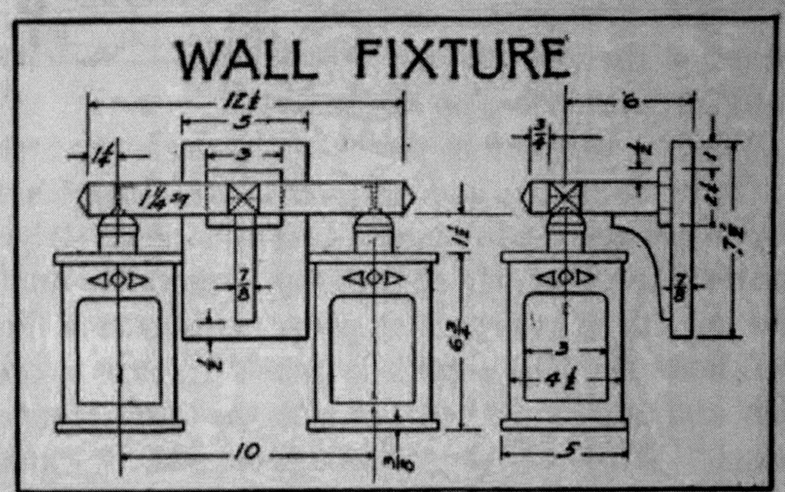

are now in order, the smaller one being mortised to match the central arm. The curved bracket remains to be shaped up, after which the whole may be put together, using glue and a few nails so placed as to be invisible. The completed wall bracket and the two shades should be suitably stained, sandpapered again, filled if the wood is open-grained, and sanded once more when dry, after which a thorough rubbing with wax completes the job.

In living-rooms with dark woodwork and paneled walls the type of wall light shown in the accompanying illustration is effective from a decorative standpoint.

LIBRARY LAMP

The illuminant for this library lamp may be either kerosene or electricity. If the former is used, procure from a dealer in manual training supplies a suitable oil pot and burner, which are made

for just this class of lamps. The pot is usually of copper and has a supporting flange around the top, so that it is only necessary to cut a large circular opening in the top of the standard and set in the pot. The burners are of the center-draft type and are of high candlepower. Of course, almost any good burner may be soldered to a tin can and arranged to give good service.

If electricity is to be used, one high power lamp set directly on the top of the standard will answer. The cord may then be carried downward and out to one side under the base.

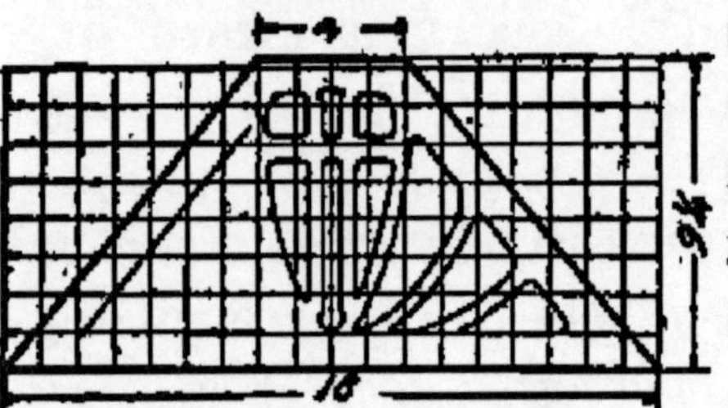

Quite the most difficult feature will be the construction of the shade. The dimensions of one of the four sections are given in the accompanying sketch. Accurately lay out the pattern on a sheet of paper and transfer it to each of the four pieces, which may be of several materials. If wood is used, the cross grain at the top and bottom must be reënforced with strips glued on the inside. Considerable care will be necessary in fitting the corner seams and in sawing out the pattern.

In making trunks, thin boards are used which are composed of three or more thicknesses of veneer. This material is very strong, does not warp, and will stand all manner of scroll sawing. Another material available is what is known as Beaver Board, which is a wood product about three-sixteenths of an inch thick and is used instead of lath and plaster in building. The choice of the material will largely depend on what is most available, and in all cases reënforcing corner strips and strips along the lower edges on the inside will be found desirable. Where the corner seams are not well fitted, a carefully applied strip of passe-partout tape will hide the defects. All edges are to be sandpapered smooth

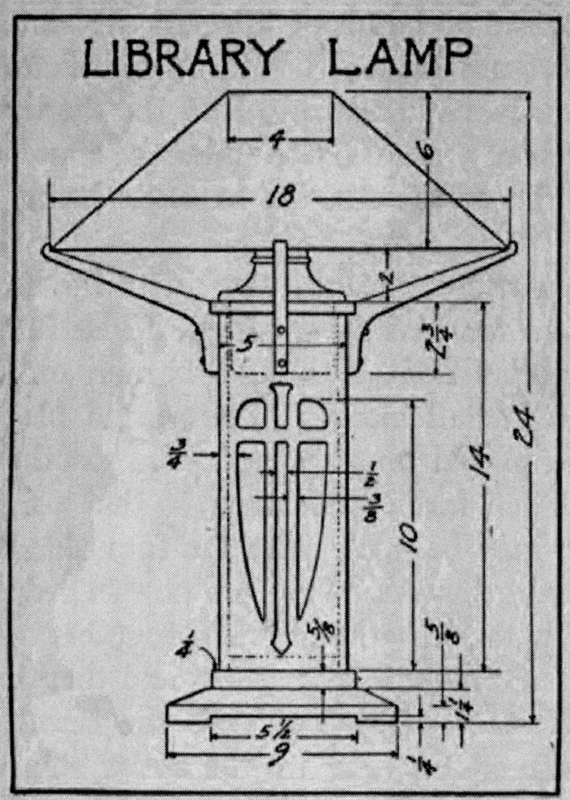

before and after painting or staining. Glass is by no means necessary for a lining, as colored papers and many fabrics answer every purpose.

Those who do not care to make the shade have three alternatives open to them. A shade may be purchased and the four supporting brackets made to fit, or one may be made of silk on a wire frame. The third plan is to secure the regular electric fixture used on lamps of this sort, which consists of a short brass standard with two sockets attached and a screw cap on top to hold the shade. In this case it is only necessary to screw the standard to the top of the woodwork, the brackets being unnecessary.

The woodwork should start with the base, which should be tenoned up squarely, beveled off on top, and then built out at the four corners on the under side with small blocks. The second block should now be placed on this, and then another one of about a half inch in thickness, so that a firmer connection may be made with the four side boards of the standard, which pieces are now in order. Trim these up to size and fit them together with bevel edges. Draw out the pattern and then transfer it to each piece. Saw out with the scroll saw and finish the edges. Set up the entire standard with glue and a very few wire brads.

The block for the top is now in order, and after sawing the large circular opening for the oil pot, secure it in place. The four brackets that support the shade are now to be made and fitted and drilled for the screws. The staining and filling should now be done, and after each coat has dried, sandpaper lightly. Finish with wax. Place brackets, oil pot, burner and shade.

CHAPTER 6

Rustic Furniture

In making rustic furniture, wood having a close firm bark should be chosen. Hickory is, of course, the most frequently used, but, as the necessary pieces cannot be ordered, one must use the most desirable wood at hand. After cutting, the pieces should be set aside in a dry place until the sap dries up.

Garden Stand.—The small garden stand is a very simple piece to make. The top is best made from two squares of inch wood, fastened together with the grain running in opposite directions, by means of screws set in from below. The three legs are then cut the same length and temporarily fitted together to determine if any slight trimming or adjustment is necessary where they cross and are attached to one another. The exact method of connecting these pieces will vary in every single case, but generally some one side will prove more advantageous for starting. If the wood is hard, small holes must first be made for the screws.

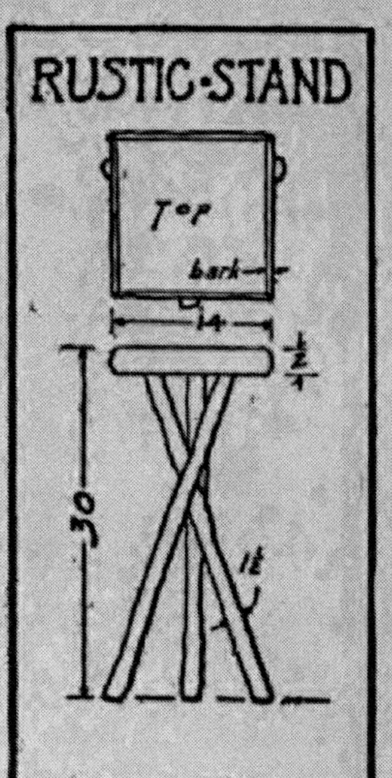

The top may be connected by boring three holes in the underside and tapering the ends of the legs to fit them tightly; or the top of each leg may be sawed off at the proper angle to allow the table-top to be set flat and then attached with a single large screw. The best method will be obvious when the crooked pieces are all arranged in place. Around the four edges of the top are nailed pieces sawed from the sides of a small branch with the bark in place. The top should be given at least one coat of oil to protect it from the weather.

Rustic Bench.—The seat of the rustic bench is made by sawing a wide slab from the side of a large log. The bark is allowed to remain on the under side, while the top is planed off smoothly. Although primarily intended for the garden, this bench may be made very attractive by finishing the top and ends as carefully as possible and then varnishing

them to bring out the grain. The contrast between the dark bark and the light polished surface is very pleasing indeed. When so finished the bench may be used indoors near the fireplace or in the den.

After the seat has been made ready and notched on the underside near each end to receive the supports, the latter should be taken up. Mark out the outline and positions of the mortises for the footrail. These, together with the tops and bottoms, must all be cut at a uniform angle,

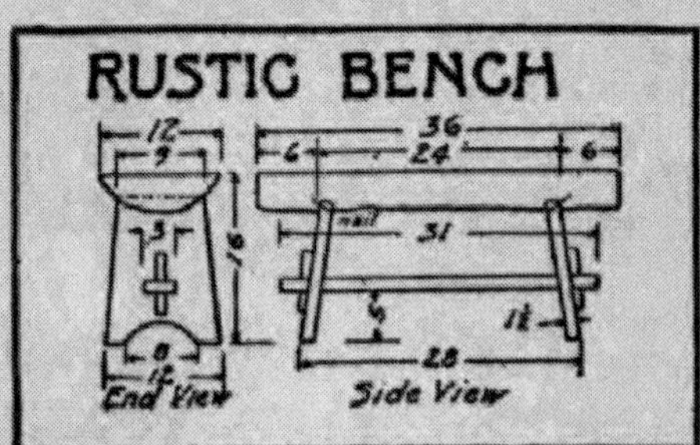

which will require some little care. Set the legs in position temporarily and then accurately determine the correct length of the foot-rail, which must then

be tenoned on the ends to match the mortises cut in the supports. Two rather large tapering keys are now to be fitted so that when they are driven home the whole will be securely clamped together. Place the seat bottom side up, and nail the supports securely into the two slots already prepared for them, after which it only remains to drive in the keys to complete the piece.

Rustic Table.—At the outset it may be well to state that, in the construction of the rustic table, it is

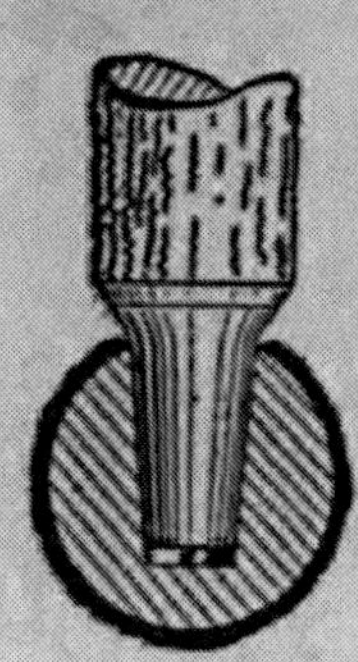

not imperative the top be circular in form, although a round one is prettier. The top is in two thicknesses, the upper one projecting about an inch beyond the lower all around. Each layer is made up of three or four boards, and the two circles are fastened together with glue and numerous screws set in from the under side. The grain of the two top sections is crossed, so that the possibility of warping is practically avoided.

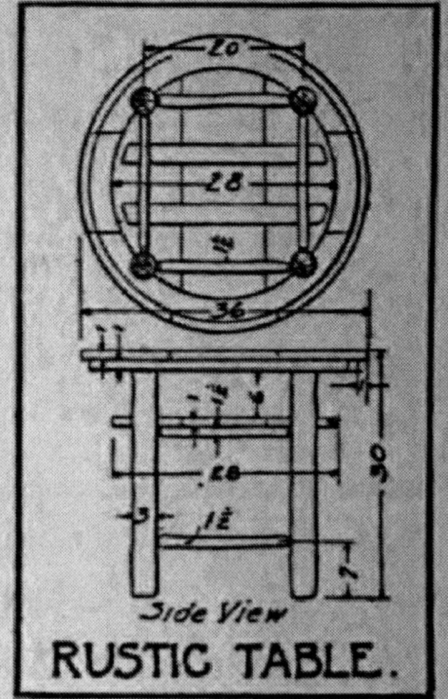

RUSTIC TABLE.

The four legs should be first cut to length and the lower ends rounded, after which they are bored for the lower and upper crosspieces, the latter for supporting the shelf. Taper the holes very slightly and then work up the eight crosspieces to match. The two legs of each side should be connected and then the two sides connected, making all of the connections as indicated in the detail sketch. The boards for the shelf should now be made ready and connected with substantial cleats across the under sides, as shown in the working drawing. Mark off the positions of the legs and then cut out circular notches so that the shelf will set down on the upper crosspieces and fit about half-way around the legs. Secure it in place with screws set in through the crosspieces. Reverse the top, place the assembled legs in position, and secure each leg to the top by means of large screws set in at an angle. A coat of oil or filler and spar varnish on the wood wherever unprotected by bark will prolong the usefulness of the table.

CHAPTER 7

Flower Boxes

Rustic Tub.—To plant flowers in a stiff looking box, a tin can or a pail, is to lose half their lovely effect when they are in bloom. We should always try to provide an attractive place for them, because much of the time the plants have no flowers and no one wishes to have an ugly box or a rusty pail standing around.

A rustic tub is suitable for large plants or even small trees, and is very easily made. Take a small tub such as butter comes in or else a wooden pail without a handle and cover the outside with slabs of wood about two inches wide with the bark on. These may be sawn from branches from three to four inches in diameter. Have them all exactly the same length and fitted closely together so that the tub is entirely hidden. If you can find some green boughs about one-half inch in diameter that will stand to be slowly bent half way around a tin can, our tub may be provided with feet, as shown in the drawing. In this case a space must be left between every other or every third slab, and the number and width of the slabs should be arranged so that the feet will come out right.

Hanging Fern Basket.—A very pretty hanging basket may be made by building up small straight sticks with the bark on in the same way that a log house is built. The size of the basket will depend largely on the size of the fern which you wish to grow, but ordinarily the sticks should be from twelve to sixteen inches long. The sizes should taper from an inch in diameter for those at the bottom to half an inch for the top ones. In starting the construction, nail four of the larger sticks together, so as to make a frame with the ends projecting about one and a half to two inches. Between the two upper sticks place a row of sticks so as to form a grating with half-inch spaces. This makes the

bottom, and in building up the sides we simply nail on two pieces running one way and then two running the other, until the desired height is reached. Always drive the nails in at an angle, so that the nails of the next layer will not interfere when they are put in. The best plan is to have the sticks all sawn to the proper length before nailing together, so that the entire attention may be given to building the sides up squarely. Two long, thin branches are now to be found and slowly bent so as to form the long handles. Nail these to the inside corners, and wire the handles together at the top—and the basket is done.

In filling such a basket with new earth it will be necessary to line the inside with moss or leaves to keep it in, but after a few waterings the whole forms into a solid mass and no trouble will be found.

Geranium Box.—For growing geraniums or other plants on window-sills or the porch rail, a long narrow box is desirable. The best way to make an attractive box for this purpose is to get from the planing mill some long strips measuring about three-quarters by one inch. Saw off thirteen pieces twenty-four inches long, and eight

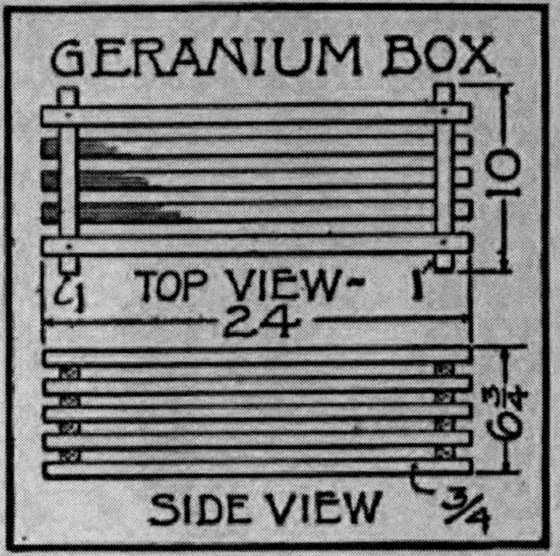

pieces ten inches long. Set down five of the long pieces and nail a short one across each end, taking due care that the long ones are evenly spaced and that all the ends project exactly the same amount. This forms the bottom, and it is a simple matter to add a pair of sides and then a pair of ends until they are all in place. Use the square to make sure that the sides and ends are going up squarely, and always nail in at an angle so that the nails of the next pair of strips will not interfere.

A good coat of dark green or brown paint will greatly preserve the box. Line with leaves or moss when first filling with new earth.

WOODEN JARDINIÈRES

Every mother loves plants and flowers, and if the young carpenter wishes to make a present that will be sure to please, just make one of these wooden flower boxes, paint it dark brown or green, and then present it with an oleander or small orange tree growing in it.

There is just one feature in the construction that will present any difficulty and that is due to the fact that the edges of the four side pieces are not exactly square with the sides. This is on account of the slant.

After studying the drawing you will notice that two of the side boards must be narrower than the other two, because they fit inside, just like the ends of any box. The only way to do, therefore, is to stand the four pieces up and then plane the edges of the two that fit inside until they fit closely. The

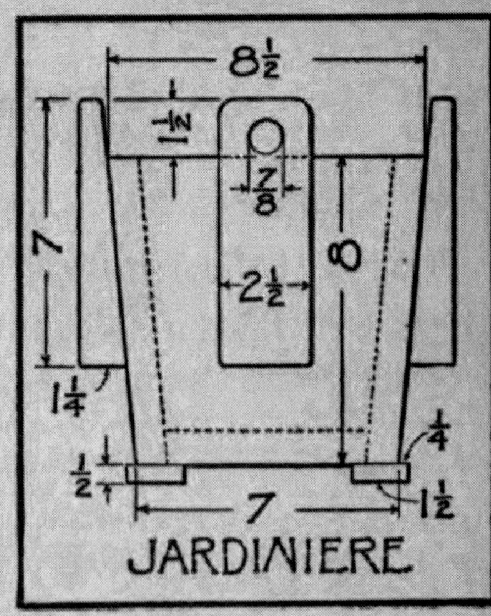

edges of the two wider pieces should not be trimmed down until all four are nailed together, when they can be worked down even with the outside. After fitting in the bottom, the four tapering pieces with the holes in them are to be made and nailed on. As these large holes come so near the ends, one had better bore them before sawing the pieces off, so as to prevent splitting. As soon as the end of the bit is felt coming through, turn the piece over and bore from the other side, so as not to tear off splinters. Nail on the small block at each corner of the bottom—and the box is done.

The construction of the second jardinière or flower box will proceed in the same way, except that we must use the fret saw to cut out the curves. After marking out the necessary one-inch squares, locate the center points marked with the black dots. Place the point of the compasses on these, and you will find that the curves shown in the working drawing will fall right in place. Saw out two sides according to the heavy lines, allowing just a little for planing off after nailing up. The other two sides will be ex-

actly the same, except that their width must be reduced by the thickness of the other two sides, otherwise our box will not be square when we look down upon it. Set the heads of the nails deeply. Apply a coat of linseed oil inside and out, and when this is dry putty up the holes over the nails. Paint brown or green as desired, giving the inside several coats as a preservative.

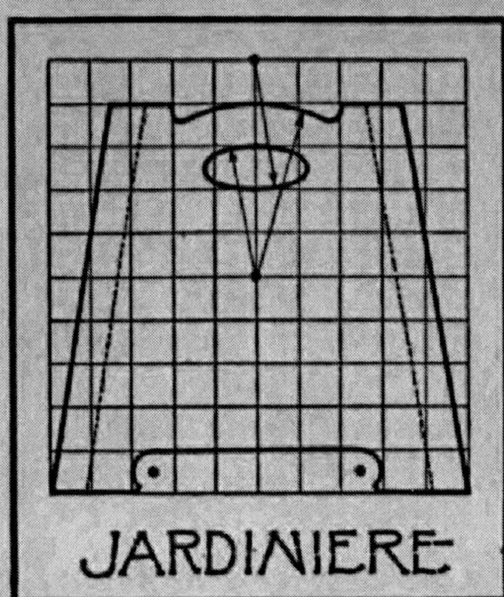

WINDOW BOXES

In making flower boxes for windows one encounters a variety of conditions. Very frequently window sills slope downward toward the outside, in which event the bottom of the box must be set at a corresponding angle.

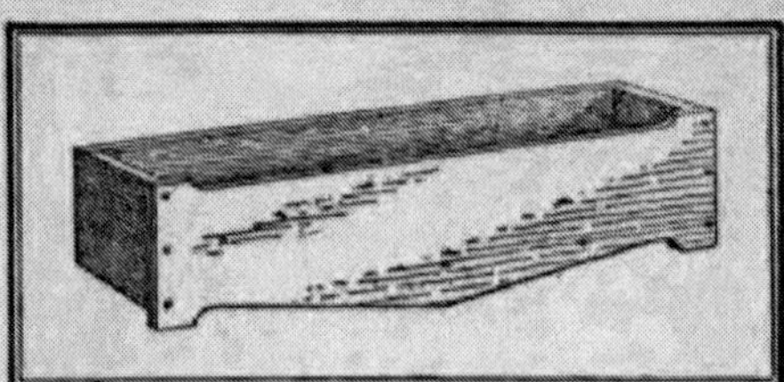

This design can be used to advantage where the sill is of such a depth that the box can be set back far enough to bring the inner surface of the front board into contact with the face of the sill. Care-

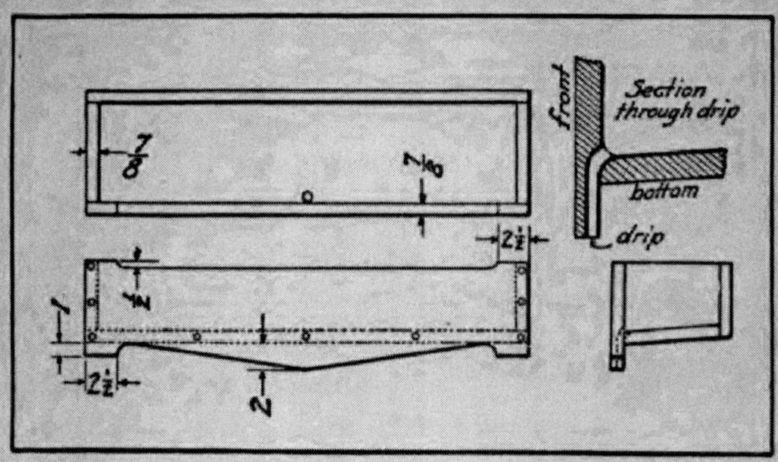

fully mark out the shape of the front board, and then work it out, finishing all edges sharp and square. The shape of the two end boards will, of course, depend on the depth and angle of the sill. In the sectional view is shown the arrangement of the spout for carrying off the drippings. In order to conceal this, a groove should be cut on the inner side of the front board, and a hole bored in the bottom. Put the whole together with screws, using those with round heads in front. Before lining with zinc, a coat of paint will add greatly to the life of the box. If one is fairly familiar with the use of the soldering iron, there ought to be no difficulty in placing this zinc lining. This, however, can be readily attended to at the tinsmith's. The upper edge of the lining should be well secured to the inside of the box by means of galvanized or tinned tacks, so as to prevent rusting. The box may be stained Flemish green or any color desired.

Where the window sill is of fair depth and has a square edge, such as a dressed-stone sill, the third design may be used to advantage. On the under side of the bottom, and at right angles thereto, a four-inch board is attached, and then three wooden brackets placed in position as shown. This arrangement makes the box appear as though supported by these brackets, whereas the actual fastening is accomplished by setting in two screw eyes in the back, which are then tied by wire to two similar screw eyes set in the wooden part of the sill. (See the sectional view.) The two front corners may seem a trifle elaborate at first sight, but in reality their construction will be found quite simple. After the tongues and grooves have all been fitted in place a wire nail should be driven in at the top and bottom, so as to hold them together. The bottom, back and ends are all plain boards, and in

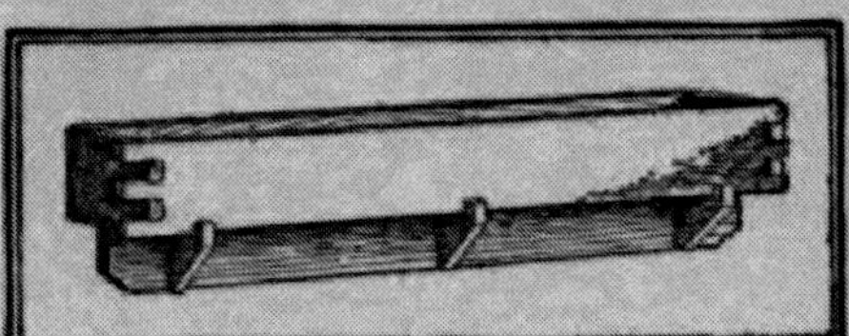

putting these together it is preferable to use screws. The arrangement of the drain is clearly indicated. This is a very attractive design and is well worth a little effort on the part of the one doing the work to make it carefully and neatly and finish it up in

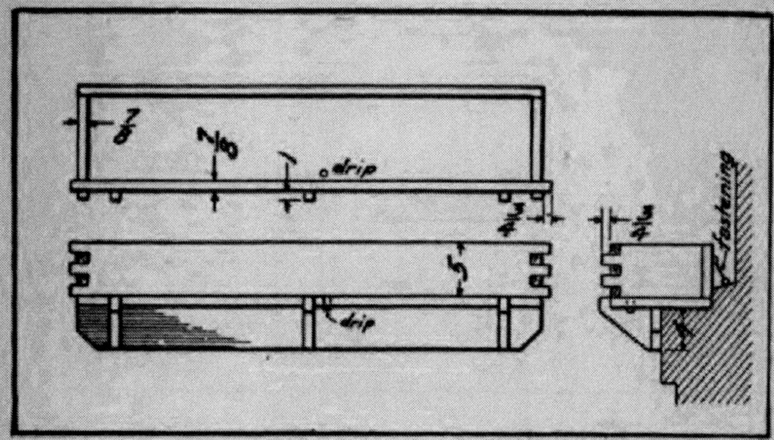

good, workmanlike fashion. Make all measurements accurate and all fittings true and exact.

When the angle of the sill is too great, or the width too little, it is usually best to make the bottom of the box square with the sides, and then provide a screw eye at each of the two front corners, so that the

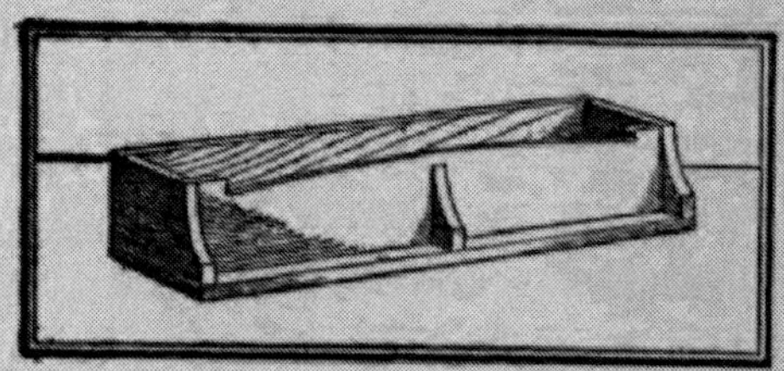

box may be held in place by means of two chains, as shown in the diagram to the left. All of the lines are quite simple, but in order to bring them out fully, care should be taken to have the edges of the various boards sharp and square. A hole should be bored in the middle of the bottom

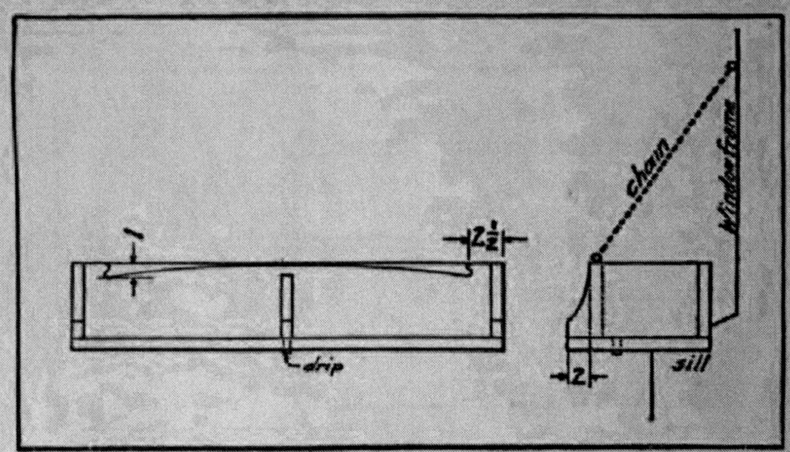

board near the front, to accommodate the drip spout, which should be soldered tightly to the zinc lining, and which should preferably extend a trifle below the bottom of the box, so as to keep the drippings away from the wood. Stain dark brown or

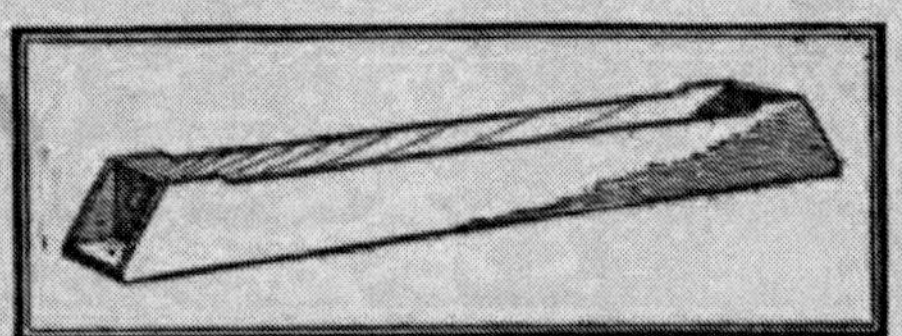

Flemish green. The depth of all these boxes may vary from four to seven inches and the width from five to twelve inches. Of course the dimensions of the window where the box will be placed will govern this. The lumber used should be about an inch in thickness.

The long narrow box is for use along the porch rail, and the construction is so simple that nothing need be said in regard thereto. To hold securely in place, a screw should be set in at each end through the projecting ends of the bottom board into the

porch rail. A good substitute for the metallic lining consists of thoroughly coating and impregnating the inside and drip holes with heavy crude oil or tar residue, such as may be obtained from the gas works. Two or more applications should be given, after each of which the box should be placed in the sun until thoroughly dry.

CHAPTER 8

Bird Houses

To entice the birds to nest about our homes two things are equally necessary—the first is to provide the proper sort of a house and the second to place it in a suitable location. A woodpecker or a flicker invariably take up lodgings at the bottom of a deep, dark hole, while the robin and the phoebe prefer lots of light, and a house to suit them must have the whole side knocked out. The same radical difference in taste is displayed in the matter of location. A catbird likes to be near the ground among shrubbery, while the house-finch, true to his name, must live high up near the eaves. It will therefore be apparent how important it is, before commencing actual construction, to make a general survey of one's neighborhood to ascertain the different kinds of birds that are available and to determine the most suitable points at which to place the new houses. In doing this one should remember that unless a great deal of space is at one's disposal it is hardly to be expected that more than one family of any species can be secured, except in the case of martins, which are noted for their social instincts. With this single exception all of our common birds have a marked dislike for others of their own species, particularly during the breeding season, although it is not uncommon to see different sorts nesting quite close together.

For some reason best known to themselves wrens and bluebirds dislike to raise a second brood in the same nest, and as these birds raise two broods each year, several nests should be provided if we wish to have the family remain with us. Most birds are naturally quarrelsome and it is always best to provide lots of houses.

It is a common error to make bird houses too ornamental, with the result that they fail to harmonize with their surroundings—a serious defect in the opinion of most birds. The inherent idea of self preservation usually results in the selection of quarters as unobtrusive as possible, and it is for this reason that a bird house made from an old log is so often found tenanted.

Log Houses.—A very successful house of this type may be made by splitting a log in two and then hollowing out the two halves with a gouge, so that a deep, pear-shaped pocket will be formed when they are put together. The log should be quite dry, five or six inches in diameter, and about two feet long. Saw the ends off at an angle so as

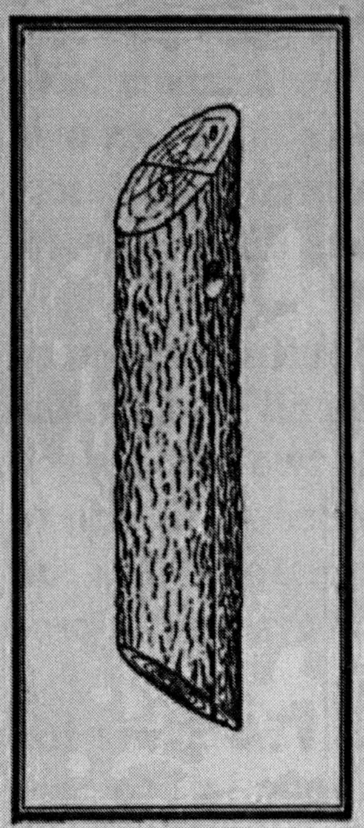

to shed the water, and fasten the two pieces together with a screw at each end. When necessary these may be removed for cleaning the nest. The accompanying diagram illustrates the proper form of cavity, which should be marked out from a pattern so that both halves will be exactly the same. The seam should be light-proof, and in order to keep out moisture it is advisable to cover the top with a piece of zinc or a shingle.

Another very successful bird house may be made from a log having a decayed center. A large opening is to be cleaned out from end to end and the top sawed off at an angle, after which a projecting lug should be formed with the saw at the lower end as illustrated. In fastening the house in place a screw should be put in through this lug and another at the top before the roof is put on. This latter should be large enough to shed the water, and the bottom is

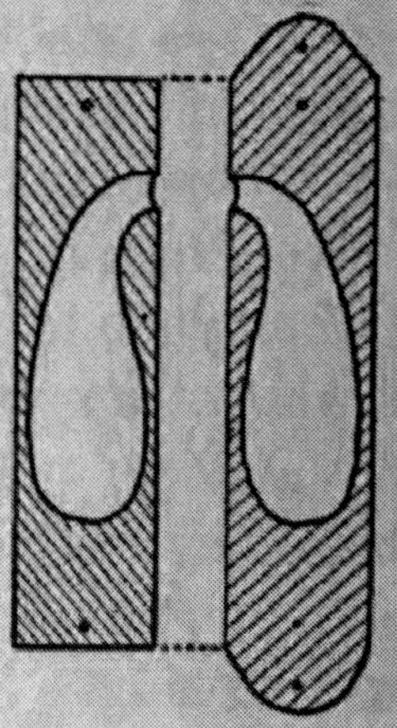

to be fitted in in a manner that will permit of its removal for cleaning. This may be accomplished by securing it in place by driving in about three nails through the sides so as to engage the bottom board. If the proper length nail is chosen and the heads allowed to project about a quarter of an inch they may be readily withdrawn when it is desired to remove the bottom.

After having placed the house, pour in a little clean sawdust to facilitate the building of the nest.

The most important consideration in the making of a bird house suitable for nesting is to have the floor space and depth of the proper dimensions, and to provide an opening of the requisite diameter at the correct distance above the bottom. The following table is taken from data compiled by the U. S. Biological Survey and will be found of great assistance in securing the proper proportions.

SPECIES	FLOOR SPACE	DEPTH	ENTRANCE ABOVE FLOOR	DIAMETER ENTRANCE	HEIGHT ABOVE GROUND
Bluebird	5 x 5	8	6	1½	5–10 ft.
Chickadee	4 x 4	8–10	8	1⅛	6–15 "
Crested flycatcher	6 x 6	8–10	8	2	8–20 "
Dipper	6 x 6	6	1	3	1–3 "
Flicker	7 x 7	16–18	16	2½	6–20 "
Hairy woodpecker	6 x 6	12–15	12	1½	12–20 "
House-finch	6 x 6	6	4	2	8–12 "
House wren	4 x 4	6–8	1–6	⅞	6–10 "
Martin	6 x 6	6	1	2½	15–20 "
Red-headed woodpecker	6 x 6	12–15	12	2	12–20 "
Tree swallow	5 x 5	6	1–6	1½	10–15 "
Tufted titmouse	4 x 4	8–10	8	1¼	6–15 "
White-breasted nuthatch	4 x 4	8–10	8	1¼	12–20 "

Woodpecker House.—For such birds as woodpeckers, nuthatches, titmice and chickadees a deep narrow nest is essential. The accompanying working drawing gives the dimensions for the largest size—that adapted to the industrious red-headed woodpecker, but the reader will have no difficulty in making the necessary reductions to bring the house into conformity with the foregoing table for the other members of this family.

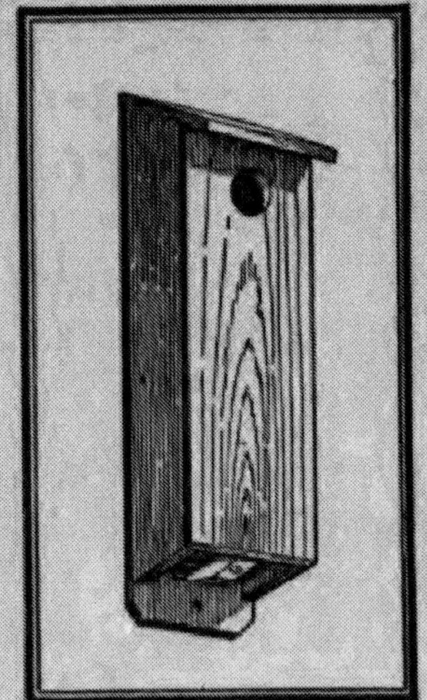

All of the pieces may be cut from two boards, if they are marked out as indicated in the drawing. Use three-quarter-inch lumber, as it is a great mistake to make bird houses of thin box material that only warps so as to make the seams gape after the

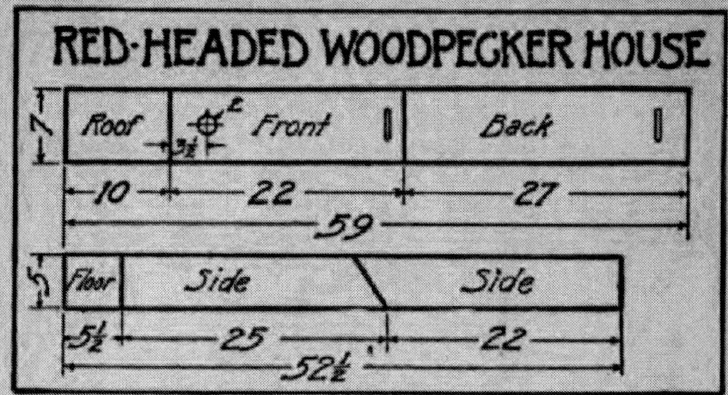

first rain. Birds will not tolerate a house with open seams or cracks.

The distinctive feature of this house is the method by which the bottom is arranged so as to be readily removable when it is desired to clean out the house in the spring for new tenants. The bottom board is made just large enough to slip inside and carries a wooden button pivoted on a screw on the underside. A square groove is cut on the inner surface of both the front and back boards, so that when the button is turned its ends will engage these grooves and hold the bottom securely in place. Birds of the woodpecker family are especially industrious and usually build a new house

WOODPECKER HOUSE

each year. It will therefore be apparent that adequate facilities for cleaning are quite necessary if we expect the same birds to return.

The construction is otherwise too simple to require comment. Nail together securely, set the heads of the nails deeply and putty over. A coat of green, dark gray or brown paint will add not only to the life but to the appearance of the house, and a simple strip run around the front will aid greatly in relieving the plainness which is unavoidable in deep houses of this sort.

When the house is to be placed in a tree, a good plan is to cover it with bark, or else construct it from pieces of wood from which the bark has not been removed.

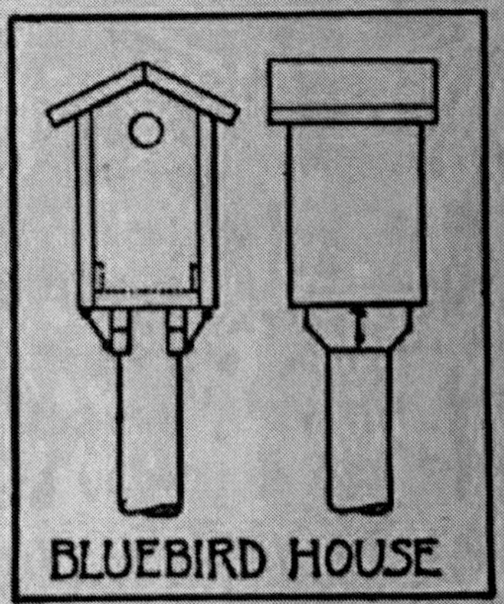

BLUEBIRD HOUSE

As a woodpecker gathers no nesting material, a little sawdust should be placed in the bottom.

Bluebird House.—The bluebird as well as the

woodpecker has a preference for nesting in a deep cavity. The accompanying sketches illustrate a house adapted to their needs, designed to be placed on a pole or on the stump of a branch in a tree. Bluebirds, it may be stated, appear to have an

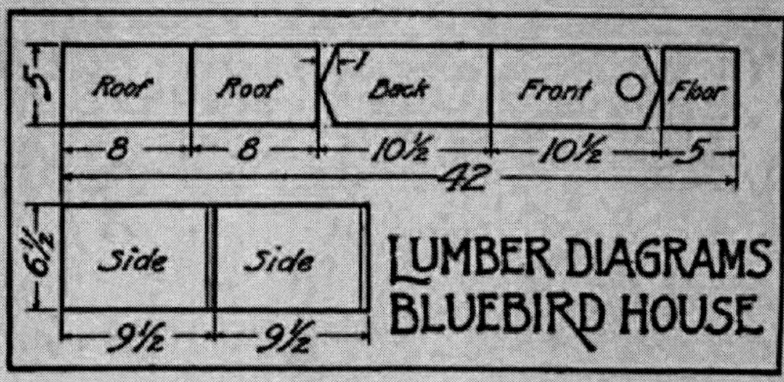

aversion for a house that is suspended from above.

The special feature in the design of this house is the provision made for cleaning—a matter too often overlooked in planning bird houses. Instead of attaching the bottom to the sides, it is securely nailed and braced on the top of a pole. The house slips on over the bottom, and is prevented from dropping down too far by four small strips nailed around the inside. A hook and eye at each side holds it securely in place, and at the same time makes it possible to quickly remove the house for cleaning.

The entire house may be readily worked out from two three-quarter-inch boards, as shown in the lumber diagram. First nail the four sides together, and then fit on the top. Fit all seams closely, and

cover the ridge with a strip of zinc or tin to shed the water. It is a good plan in sawing out the entrance to make the outside diameter somewhat larger than the inside, as this will tend to keep the water from trickling inside during a driving rain.

This house may also be painted a quiet shade of gray, green or brown, or else covered with bark. Always place it with the back toward the prevailing winds if these are noticeable.

House for Jenny Wren.—The wren is usually regarded as one of the birds most easily enticed into a bird house. They will sometimes take up quarters in an old tomato can set on a fence post, if the open end is closed and a small entrance is provided instead. They prefer considerable shade and usually locate from six to ten feet above the ground. A house adapted to their needs will also answer for a house-finch if placed near the eaves of a building.

In the accompanying illustrations a simple design is presented for a wren house, which has a form of entrance that seems to appeal to the bird's idea of safety. The entrance is through the gable, which is left open, and then through a square open-

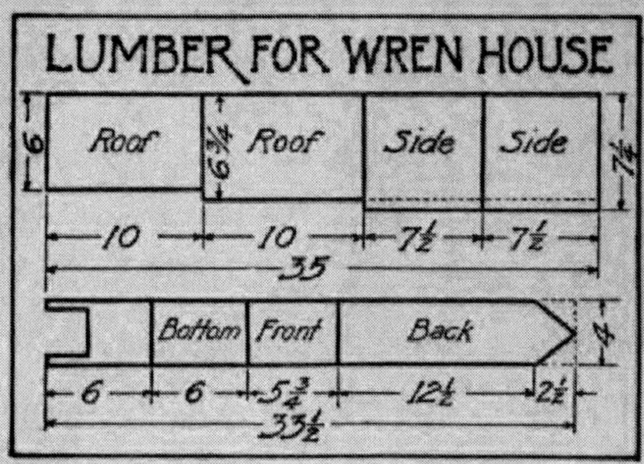

ing cut in what may be termed the rear of the attic floor.

The lumber diagram shows exactly how to cut each piece. Only two three-quarter-inch boards are necessary, and the only feature of the construction that will require any particular care will be the fitting of the roof. Before putting this on, however, a small strip should be nailed on each of the side walls to support the attic floor, which is not to be nailed in place. This arrangement permits of its removal when it is desired to clean out the nest.

Nesting Shelves.—The phœbe and barn swallow

prefer to nest under the eaves, and require nothing more than a little nook or corner. The accompanying sketches illustrate a suitable form of nesting shelf, the construction of which is very simple. If several of these are to be put up, make one or more with one side open as well as the front.

Nest Shelter.—A still more open form of nesting place is the "shelter." When placed in the shrubbery, song sparrows, catbirds and brown thrashers are likely to use it. Robins may also appropriate it when placed on one of the branches of a large tree.

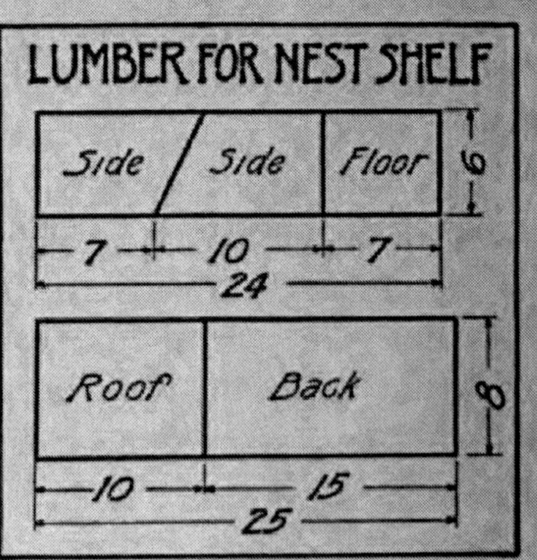

The lumber diagrams show just what lumber to order, and how to cut each piece. As in the other houses three-quarter inch material is used. First shape up the ends, sawing out the entrances with a fret saw, and then prepare the bottom, sawing the ends off perfectly square. Nail these securely together, and then put on the roof boards,

covering the ridge with a strip of zinc or tin. A small strip of wood should then be nailed on along each of the two sides to hold the nesting material in position.

When placed in the brush this nest is best secured on the end of a short pole set firmly in the ground.

Martins.—As previously stated martins are by far the most social birds we have. They always live in colonies, and only an apartment house will suit them. To make an attractive martin house is quite an undertaking, and while space is not available for plans and descriptions, it may be stated that to be successful ample provision should be made for cleaning, and the house should be placed about twenty feet from a building and on a pole fifteen to twenty feet high.

In conclusion it will not be amiss to remind the reader that there are other attractions for birds in addition to providing suitable houses. Thus a food shelter, where lettuce leaves, seeds, grain, or some suet may be placed, is particularly desirable in cold weather when food is scarce. In summer time a

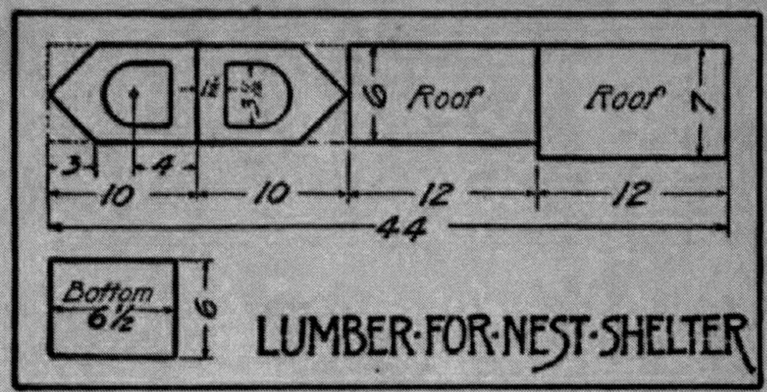

bird bath, consisting of a shallow pond two or three feet across, is a great attraction, and it is always advisable to provide nesting material such as bits of string, small feathers and tiny scraps of rag.

THE END

Lightning Source UK Ltd.
Milton Keynes UK
172445UK00006B/62/P

9 781145 674790